Slavery as Moral Problem

FACETS

Selected Titles in the Facets Series

Slavery as Moral Problem

In the Early Church
and Today

Jennifer A. Glancy

Fortress Press
Minneapolis

SLAVERY AS MORAL PROBLEM
In the Early Church and Today

Cover image: Slave monument Zanzibar © Eric Lafforgue
Cover design: Ivy Palmer Skrade

Library of Congress Cataloging-in-Publication Data
Glancy, Jennifer A.
 Slavery as moral problem : in the early church and today / Jennifer A. Glancy.
    p. cm.
 Includes bibliographical references.
 ISBN 978-0-8006-9670-2 (alk. paper)
 1. Slavery and the church. 2. Church and social problems. I. Title.
 HT913.G525 2011
 241'.675—dc22
                                    2010049010

Manufactured in the U.S.A.

15   14   2   3   4   5   6   7   8   9   10

Contents

Introduction

Was slavery a moral problem for the first Christians? Regardless of how we respond, why should the realities of ancient slaveholding raise moral questions for Christians in the twenty-first century?

This brief volume attempts to highlight the urgency of these questions. It also suggests ways in which early Christian writings that touch on slavery may offer resources for confronting ethical dilemmas of our own day.

Rome was a slaveholding empire. No one who lived in the empire could avoid participating in its slave-dependent economy. According to the Gospels, Jesus of Nazareth had contact with slaves—and with slaveholders. Jesus' parables and other sayings refer often, and casually, to slaves and masters. The first Christian communities included slaves. They also included slaveholders. In the third millennium Christians comfortably acknowledge that some early Christians were slaves. We are far less comfortable acknowledging that some early Christians enslaved others.

Paul writes that all who have been baptized are united in Christ: "There is no longer Jew or Greek, there is no longer slave or free, there is no longer male and female" (Gal. 3:28). On that basis many readers of Paul would like to conclude that the early Christian community effectively transcended differences between slaves and slaveholders. Not so.

Baptism did not transform everyday relations of slavery, even when both slave and master worshiped in the same congregation. This was true in the first century, when the gospel first began to be preached around the Mediterranean. It continued to be true throughout the fourth century, when Christianity was established as the official religion of the empire.

Perhaps it seems incongruous that the early Christian movement sanctioned slaveholding. After all, ancient Christian communities remembered that Jesus taught his followers they should be slaves to one another (Mark 10:43-44; Matt. 20:26-27). This teaching could even be said to be at the heart of the gospel message.

Early Christian perpetuation of slaveholding values may also seem incongruous because we know how important nineteenth-century Christians were in pushing for the abolition of slavery in the North Atlantic. The teachings of Jesus and of the early church figured importantly in the articulation of a coherent antislavery stance.

A focus on Christian resistance to slavery and the incompatibility of slavery with Christian values may seem more hopeful than acknowledgment of the pervasive and insidious impact of slavery on the church. Is it contradictory to refer to Christian slavery? Today, many would say yes. However, in antiquity, many church leaders were slaveholders. Church policy supported the rights of slaveholders. To correct the distorting traces of slaveholding values that linger in Christian thought and practice, it is first necessary to acknowledge how thoroughly early Christians internalized the values of the wider society.

I approach the study of slavery and early Christianity both as a historian and as a Christian. The history of early Christian slavery is of more than antiquarian interest. American Christian communities who advocate for reparations for slavery may be sobered—but nonetheless emboldened—by learning about slavery in early Christianity. In addition, although we tend to refer to slavery in the past tense, slavery remains a pressing global problem. An end to contemporary slavery is a goal for many Christian activists. Attention to ancient Christian voices that challenged the legitimacy of slaveholding values may inspire Christians who are working to end slavery now.

More generally, attention to the ancient Christians who bought, sold, and whipped slaves invites reflection on systems of exploitation and oppression in which we participate today. As I write about the dynamics of slavery in early Christianity, I wonder which practices of contemporary American life will be rejected by future generations as immoral. On a personal level I wonder how I can begin to recognize and act against such immorality, even when I benefit from it.

In antiquity the vast majority of Jesus' followers—at least those who left any written record—did not regard slaveholding as morally repugnant. Today, Christians regard slaveholding as incompatible with the good news Jesus preached. Our task is not to judge the past by the standards of the present. Rather, our task is to trace the insidious impact of slaveholding values on Christian thought and practice so that we may better witness to the gospel of freedom.

Prison System, Welfare System, Judicial System

1

Jesus and Slavery

What was it like to be a slave in Galilee? A slave might handle large sums of money for an owner, yet that owner could, at will, torture the slave. A slave might function as the trusted agent of a slaveholder, but his low status nonetheless left him vulnerable to physical abuse by those he encountered. Some slaves were overseers, exerting physical control over lower-ranking slaves. Lower-ranking slaves endured the violence not only of slaveholders but also of slave overseers. Food for slaves was often doled out as rations, or else slaves waited until slaveholders finished eating before consuming the leftovers. Slaves labored in agriculture. Slaves, male and female, labored in domestic settings. Some slaves enjoyed their owners' trust. Perhaps all slaves lived in fear.

These glimpses of slave life are taken from the parables attributed to Jesus of Nazareth. The casual frequency of Jesus' reliance on slave imagery is a clue that we should pay careful attention to the slaves and slaveholders who populated Jesus' world.

Can we imagine Jesus in the midst of a slaveholding world? It is important to do so, because we may otherwise overlook or misinterpret the slaves who populate his parables. In his parables, Jesus relied on everyday images. His parables featured fishermen. They featured women cleaning house. They featured sheep and shepherds, leaven and bread baking. They also featured, prominently and repeatedly, slaves and slaveholders.

Despite the familiarity of the parables, the slaves who populate the parables seem somehow unfamiliar. The King James Bible typically translates the Greek word *doulos* as "servant" rather than "slave." For many Christians the phrase "Well done, good and faithful servant" resonates in a way that the phrase "Well done, good and faithful slave" does not. The Greek is not ambiguous, however. In a wide range of sayings, Jesus refers to *douloi*, slaves.

Christians today struggle to make sense of the ways Jesus spoke about slaves and masters. Where's the good news? In assessing the place of slave imagery in Jesus' sayings, we need to account both for the battered slaves in his parables and for his mandate to his followers to become "slaves of all."

Slavery in Galilee and Judea

Spartacus would not have found in Palestine the concentration of slaves he found in Italy in the first century B.C.E.—a concentration sufficient to muster an army. Nonetheless, slavery existed in Galilee and Judea. Small landholders owned a few slaves. Some householders owned a few slaves for domestic labor, gardening, marketing, and service as financial agents. Slaveholders incurred no penalties for sexual relations with their slaves, nor did slaves enjoy protection from unwanted sexual advances by their owners.

The Herodian household owned a vast number of slaves. Slaves and freedpersons associated with the Herodian household would have mingled with the free peasants of Galilee. Military officials and other occupying authorities brought slaves with them to Palestine. In Palestine occupying forces continued to buy and sell slaves.

The forms of slavery familiar to Jesus were more widely familiar throughout the eastern reaches of the Roman Empire. This may surprise those familiar with biblical law. The Torah stipulates that Israelites could not own fellow Israelites as chattel slaves. Rather, an Israelite could only hold a fellow Israelite as a bondsman or bondswoman for six years, with an expectation of freedom in the seventh year (cf. Exod. 21:1-11; Deut. 15:12-18; and Lev. 25:35-46). Even in the sixth century B.C.E., however, Jeremiah castigated the people of Jerusalem for ignoring this commandment (Jer. 34:8-16). We have no evidence from the Hellenistic or Roman periods to suggest that biblical slave law governed Palestinian practices.[1] Even if some pious Jews freed Jewish bondsmen and bondswomen in the seventh year of servitude, that practice would not have benefited Gentile slaves owned by Jews, nor would it have benefited Gentile or Jewish slaves owned by Gentiles in Palestine.

To be a slave in the Greco-Roman world was a harsh fate, regardless of whether the slaveholder was Gentile or Jew. Gentile, Jewish, and Christian moralists were critical of cruel slaveholders, but slaveholders suffered no penalties for cruel actions. Furthermore, even moralists approved of regular disciplinary violence against slaves. Sometime in the second century B.C.E., the Jewish sage Ben Sira wrote these words:

> Fodder and a stick and burdens for a donkey; bread and discipline and work for a slave. Set your slave to work, and you will find rest; leave his hands idle, and he will seek liberty. Yoke and thong will bow the neck, and for a wicked slave there are racks and tortures.

> Put him to work, in order that he may not be idle, for idleness teaches much evil. Set him to work, as is fitting for him, and if he does not obey, make his fetters heavy. Do not be overbearing toward anyone, and do nothing unjust. If you have but one slave, treat him like yourself, because you have bought him with blood. If you have but one slave, treat him like a brother, for you will need him as you need your life. If you ill-treat him, and he leaves you and runs away, which way will you go to seek him? (33:25-33)

Ben Sira advises the reader against unjust and overbearing behavior, yet his advice is paired with an injunction to rely on force to control slaves. Apparently, ancient and modern audiences have different understandings of what constitutes "unjust and overbearing behavior."

Ben Sira does advocate leniency for the slaveholder humble enough to own but one slave. Such leniency is justified on the basis of self-interest. The humble slaveholder would be hard up if the lone slave ran away. Similar advice can be found in the words of Gentile moralists of the era. We have no evidence to suggest that the slaves Jesus encountered were treated differently from the slaves in other eastern provinces.

So was there anything distinctive about Jewish slavery? Documents and inscriptions suggest that, outside of Palestine, synagogues sometimes purchased the freedom of Jewish slaves.[2] Perhaps Diaspora communities were especially concerned to strengthen their communities by rescuing fellow Jews.

What about rabbinic law? In many respects, Jewish slave law was similar to Roman slave law. An important exception: rabbinic law was more inclined than Roman law to penalize a slaveholder who caused the death of his or her slave.[3] However, because rabbinic law was codified centuries after the destruction of the Jerusalem temple, it tells us little about the practices of Jesus' fellow Jews in the early first century.

Intriguingly, several first-century Jewish writers mention a group of Jews who rejected the practice of slaveholding. The Alexandrian philosopher Philo and the historian Josephus both claimed that a Jewish group known as the Essenes refused to be slaveholders. Philo asserted that Essenes repudiated the institution of slavery because they believed it violated the common humanity of those involved.[4]

The reports of Josephus and Philo can help us imagine what Jesus knew about slavery. First, we should note that both Josephus and Philo accepted Jewish slaveholding as the norm. Thus, the principled rejection of slaveholding demanded attention. Second, the reports of Josephus and Philo raise the possibility that Jesus of Nazareth might also have heard rumors about a group of Jews who questioned the morality of slaveholding. How might such rumors have influenced him?

Growing up in Nazareth, Jesus would likely have been familiar with the fate of the nearby Galilean town of Sepphoris. After the death of Herod the Great in 4 B.C.E., a Galilean named Judas led an armed insurrection against royal strongholds around Sepphoris. The campaign was short-lived. Three Roman legions crushed the uprising. In their brutal suppression of the rebels, the Romans crucified two thousand men in the vicinity of Jerusalem. In Galilee, Josephus tells us, the Romans sold the entire population of Sepphoris into slavery.[5]

In Galilee as in other parts of the Roman Empire, slavery was both a mundane and an ominous reality. While Jesus might have heard tales of a group of Jews called Essenes who repudiated slaveholding, it is still more likely that he heard tales of Galilean Jews dragged into the Diaspora to be sold as slaves.

Jesus in a Slaveholding World

We do not know the name of the slaveholder quartered in Capernaum who reportedly sought Jesus' help in healing a household member, an incident variously reported in Matthew, Luke, and in what I take to be a variation, in John (Matt. 8:5-13; Luke 7:1-10; John 4:46-54). In all three Gospels, the healing is presented as a benefit to the slaveholder. The tradition records no words of admonition to the slaveholder, nor is there an injunction to the slaveholder to free a slave or slaves in return for the healing.

The accounts differ but each identifies the slaveholder as a military or royal official, a telling detail. In Galilee, Jesus would have encountered slaves associated with the Herodian household and security forces. In Judea, Jesus would have encountered slaves belonging to the members of the Roman military, slaves who might have been purchased anywhere in the empire.

In John, Jesus is reported to be in Cana when a royal official from Capernaum begs Jesus to go to Capernaum to heal the official's son. Promising that the son will live, Jesus tells the official to go on his way. On his way back to Capernaum, the official encounters his slaves coming to meet him with word of the boy's recovery (John 4:46-54).

In the Gospel of Matthew, the incident takes place in Capernaum. A centurion approaches Jesus to ask him to heal the centurion's *pais*, a word that may refer to a child, a slave, or even to a young male lover.[6] The centurion claims that he is unworthy to have Jesus in his house but expresses a belief that Jesus could heal the *pais* by speaking a healing word. The centurion identifies himself as a slaveholder: "For I also am a man under authority, with soldiers under me; and I say to one, 'Go,' and he goes, and to another, 'Come,' and he comes, and to my slave, 'Do this,' and the slave does it" (Matt. 8:9).

The Gospel of Luke narrates a more detailed version of the incident (Luke 7:1-10). Luke reports that a centurion in Capernaum has a valued or honored slave who is ill. The centurion sends a delegation of Jewish elders to Jesus to beseech his assistance. The elders beg Jesus on behalf of the Jewish community. The centurion, they say, built the synagogue, presumably the synagogue where Jesus taught and healed (Luke 4:31-37). Jesus accompanies the elders to the centurion's house, but on the way they encounter a second delegation, this time a delegation of the centurion's friends. The friends deliver the message that in Matthew the centurion delivers himself. The centurion considers himself unworthy to have Jesus in his home but entreats Jesus to speak a healing word. The friends report the words spoken by the centurion himself in Matthew: "For I also am a man set under authority, with soldiers under me; and I say . . . to my slave, 'Do this,' and the slave does it" (Luke 7:8).

The centurion is strikingly concerned for the well-being of his slave. Such paternalism is consistent with imperial slaveholding ideology. The centurion's message suggests not so much humility as the deference of an authoritarian man to the greater authority of Jesus. Both in Matthew and in Luke, the centurion is said to call Jesus *Kyrie. Kyrie* is often translated *Lord*, but in this context, it is more appropriately translated *Master*. The centurion, a military man, acknowledges the authority of those hierarchically above him and the obedience of those hierarchically beneath him. Jesus ranks among those above him in power. Jesus responds positively to the centurion's declaration of trust in the chain of command: "Not even in Israel have I found such faith" (Luke 7:9). The slave is healed.

Did Jesus in fact reach out in compassion to a slave-holding official of Capernaum, or did later tradition invent the episode in all its variants? Jesus enjoyed a reputation as a healer, and I expect there were historical incidents that engendered that reputation. What seems important is that three Evangelists have no qualms about reporting Jesus' approving interaction with a slaveholder. To an extent that is difficult for us to appreciate, slaves and slaveholders were an unquestioned part of the landscape of the Roman Empire, even in its remoter provinces.

The presence of slaves in their masters' retinues was so commonplace as to escape comment. Consider an incident reported toward the end of each canonical Gospel. Each Gospel reports that during Jesus' arrest, the ear of the high priest's slave is severed. However, in describing the arresting party, none of the Gospels bothers to mention that slaves are present. Consistent with patterns of narration we find from other sources in the Greco-Roman world, the inclusion of slaves in such cohorts is so ordinary as to escape notice. Had the slave's ear not been severed, no Gospel would note his presence.

The Gospels are peppered with reports of Jesus in conversation, often tense, with those threatened by him. His interlocutors are variously identified as scribes, Pharisees, and teachers of the Law. Are these men slaveholders? They are not identified as such, and we should not assume they are. But they might be.

The implicit assumption that they are *not* slave-holders is problematic. Jesus moved in a world of slaveholders and slaves, a world where slavery was an everyday reality. The Evangelists mention the presence of a slave in the cohort that arrests Jesus only because of a violent incident involving the slave. Why bother to mention slaves who might accompany Pharisees or scribes? Why bother to mention that some of these individuals owned slaves?

The situation is no different with those drawn to Jesus for wisdom or healing. I have already commented on Jesus' readiness to respond to the plea of a royal official or centurion who was a slaveholder. Here is a brief list of some other figures in the Gospels who, if they were historical figures, could plausibly have been slaveholders: the leader of a synagogue, identified in Mark and Luke as Jairus, who requests healing for his daughter (Matt. 9:18-25; Mark 5:21-34; Luke 8:40-55); the rich young man who approaches Jesus to ask about eternal life (Matt. 19:16-22; Mark 10:17-22; in Luke 18:18-25, a rich ruler); Zacchaeus (Luke 19:1-10); the Syrophoenician woman (Mark 7:24-30; cf. Matt. 15:21-28); and Nicodemus (who first appears in John 3:1-10).

This list is not exhaustive. Could a Pharisee who invited Jesus to dine at his home be a slaveholder? How would it affect our reconstructions of the circles around Jesus to take into account the slaveholding population of first-century Palestine?

Although Jesus is reported to instruct Zacchaeus and the rich young man to divest themselves of their wealth in part or whole, he gives no special instructions to free whatever slaves they own. Was there a "historical Jairus"? A "historical Zacchaeus"? If not, I find it perfectly plausible that Jesus interacted with slaveholding peers of Jairus and Zacchaeus. The Gospels do not describe Jairus and Zacchaeus as slaveholders, but then we would not expect them to do so.

Perhaps most problematically, Luke implies that some of the apostles were slaveholders. In Luke 17, Jesus speaks to his disciples. The apostles petition Jesus to enhance their faith. Jesus replies that if the apostles had the faith of a mustard seed, they could move mountains. Still speaking to the apostles, he continues:

> Which one of you who has a slave that plows or tends sheep, when he returns home from the field, would say to him, "Come here at once and take your place at the table?" Would you not rather say to him, "Prepare supper for me, put on your apron and serve me while I eat and drink; later, you may eat and drink?" Do you thank the slave for doing what was commanded? So you also, when you have done all that you were ordered to do, say, "We are worthless slaves; we have done only what we ought to have done." (Luke 17:7-10)

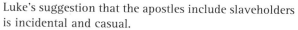

Luke's suggestion that the apostles include slaveholders is incidental and casual.

A trend in commentaries is to analyze this parable without recognition of its second-person address, an address that, in context, is directed to the disciples and more immediately to the apostles. Joseph Fitzmyer at least acknowledges the difficulty: "Details in the parable proper (having a servant, a farm with fields to be plowed and sheep to be tended) seem out of place if the parable were originally addressed either to 'disciples' or 'apostles'."[7]

Such details seem out of place to us but not to Luke. In 18:28, Peter reminds Jesus that he and his companions left their households to follow Jesus. Did some of those households include slaves? The two volumes of Luke-Acts are colored by Luke's cosmopolitan knowledge of the wider empire. Still, though I find it difficult to imagine the apostles as (former) slaveholders, it gives me pause to consider that Luke, so much closer than I am to the everyday realities of Jesus' world, sees nothing amiss in an off-the-cuff suggestion that some of Jesus' close followers might have had experience giving orders to slaves.

If Jesus interacted with slaveholders, he surely interacted with slaves as well. Again, one can imagine that some of the slaves and former slaves with whom Jesus interacted would not be identified as such. Luke claims that Jesus was supported by, among others, Joanna, who was the wife of Herod's steward Chuza (Luke 8:1-3). Stewards were often freedmen or slaves, and a steward's wife was likely to share his social status.

Joanna does not seem to be impoverished, but one would expect the wife of Herod's steward to have some resources at her disposal. Without concluding that Joanna was in fact of servile status—more likely a freedwoman than a slave, given her liberty to accompany Jesus—Luke's report that she traveled in Jesus' company opens the possibility that Jesus was in regular conversation with slaves and freedpersons associated with the Herodian household.

Much of this is, admittedly, speculative. However, we should keep in mind that ancient sources did not mention that an individual was a slaveholder unless that fact was immediately relevant. As a result, there was no reason for the Evangelists to name figures such as Nicodemus or Zacchaeus as slaveholders. I do not think we should assume they were—but it's at least as problematic to assume they were not. Likewise, we have little way of knowing whether other named or unnamed figures in the Gospels should be understood as slaves.

Slavery in the Parables of Jesus

Jesus' reliance on the imagery of slavery is perhaps the most important reason to situate him in a slaveholding landscape. Slaves appear in every branch of the Jesus-sayings tradition. The Gospels of Mark and John preserve sayings attributed to Jesus that feature slaves. So does the extracanonical *Gospel of Thomas.* Slaves are prominent in the parables of Q, the hypothetical early Christian document that can be defined as material common to Matthew and Luke but absent from Mark. Slaves are featured in parables found uniquely in Matthew or Luke.

Some parables attributed to Jesus turn on interactions between masters and slaves. In many of those parables, at least in the versions transmitted by the Evangelists, the master or slaveholder figuratively represents God. In other parables—for example, the parable of the prodigal son—slaves appear as incidental actors. The details about slave life that we glean from the parables are consistent with other kinds of evidence regarding slavery throughout the Empire.

Jesus' parables do not represent the full spectrum of slave life in the Roman Empire. For example, the parables do not depict slaves consigned to the harshest labors, such as laboring in mines. Nor do Jesus' parables feature prostitutes, who were frequently slaves. Keeping in mind these restrictions, we may infer from the parables that a slave's lot was not the most miserable fate in the Roman Empire.

Based on Jesus' parables, for example, we may infer that slaves did not eat as well as their owners. In one Lukan parable, Jesus refers to a slave who is tasked with giving out rations to fellow slaves (12:42). In another Lukan parable, to which I have already referred, Jesus suggests that a slaveholder would routinely expect a slave who had been working outdoors all day to delay his own dinner until he had served his master (17:7-9). Nevertheless, as we may infer from the parable of the rich man and Lazarus, many slaves enjoyed higher caloric intakes than beggars, who would hunger even for scraps (Luke 16:19-21).

The relationship of "slaves" to "the poor" requires investigation. The lot of a free poor person was often miserable. Likewise, the lot of a slave was often miserable. Still, it is revealing that throughout the empire, poor persons who were legally free lived in horror at the prospect of enslavement. Material conditions were desperate for many in first-century Palestine before the Jewish War, yet the population was terrorized and debilitated by the large-scale enslavement that resulted from that war. We have no evidence that any man who saw his wife dragged off to be sold as a slave said, "I'm glad she'll have a good meal." Men chained on the auction block did not measure up prospective buyers as patrons.

In writing of the rebel leader Eleazar speaking to the defenders of Masada, Josephus famously attributed to Eleazar words that proclaim, in effect, death before slavery: "Is a man to see his wife led off to violation, to hear the voice of his child crying 'Father!' when his own hands are bound?"[8] One reason a husband would dread seeing his wife taken in slavery was that a female slave was considered the sexual property of her owner. According to Josephus, because the men at Masada feared slavery more than death, they killed their wives and children and then themselves. Eleazar's speech is invented. The sentiment, however, is not. Slaves were considered without honor; to be a slave was shameful. This was a powerful concept in a society predicated on the dynamics of honor and shame. Throughout the empire, many preferred an empty belly to a ration of grain doled out by an overseer.

Luke

To give a better sense of the variety of ways in which slaves figure in the sayings tradition, let us consider a handful of parables from Luke. How do the Lukan parables help us think about the relationship between the categories of "the poor" and "slaves"? In the parable of the dinner party, the master orders his slaves to invite guests to a dinner (Luke 14:16-24; cf. Matt. 22:1-10). When the first guests decline, the master tells his slaves to deliver invitations to the poor, the disabled, and the shabby folk in roads and lanes. Still, the master does not ask the slaves themselves to join the party, reinforcing status distinctions between slaves and destitute free persons. Some slaves were not as materially deprived as the poorest free persons, yet the system of slavery nonetheless accorded slaves a lower status.

A similar dynamic colors the parable commonly known as the Prodigal Son (Luke 15:11-24). The son grew up on an estate that includes both hired hands and slaves. Hungry in a foreign land, the son nostalgically recalls his father's well-fed hired hands. When he returns to his father's estate, the father calls his slaves and says, "'Quickly, bring out a robe—the best one—and put it on him; put a ring on his finger and sandals on his feet.'" The parable ultimately returns the son to a position of respect within the family. He is honorably garbed and honorably shod. The dignity and uniqueness of a son's position is reinforced by the presence of family slaves, stooping to fasten sandals on the son's hard-traveled feet.

Slaveholders relied on slaves to manage funds and even to manage other slaves. The prerogatives of those enslaved agents or managers could be considerable. In Luke's parable of the slave overseer (12:42-48; cf. Matt. 24:45-51), the overseer, who distributes food rations to other household slaves in the slaveholder's absence, has access to the storerooms. In his owner's absence, he eats and drinks to excess, and he abuses his power over the other slaves.

This is the only canonical parable to feature female slaves. The overseer beats both male and female slaves. The parable illustrates the access some slaves enjoyed both to power and to material resources. We should note that most slaves in the parable do not enjoy such access. Although the parable centers on the slave manager, the parable presents him as an atypical slave.

We should not leave Luke's version of the parable of the slave overseer without commenting on its final vision of punishment—not its gruesome allusion to dismemberment (the angry slaveholder cuts the overseer in pieces) but its disturbing summary of the routine discipline of slaves: "That slave who knew what his master wanted, but did not . . . do what was wanted will receive a severe beating. But the one who did not know and did what deserved a beating will receive a light beating" (Luke 12:47-48). These words that Luke attributes to Jesus crystallize ancient expectations regarding the vulnerability of slaves to disciplinary violence.

Matthew

Two facets of slavery evident in the parables of Luke are still more evident in the parables of Matthew. The first is that many slaves in the Roman Empire acted as agents or managers for their owners, as illustrated by Luke's parable of the slave overseer. When we turn to Matthew, we find that almost all parables in which slaves figure feature slaves who act as agents or play managerial roles. Second, in Luke's parable of the slave overseer, Jesus gives a pithy summary of slaves' routine expectations of violence: those who knowingly defy the slaveholder are beaten severely, but even those who unwittingly fail to please the slaveholder should expect to be bruised. The parables of Matthew emphasize this liability of the slave to abuse and punishment. Although the agricultural slaves of the parable of the weeds and wheat escape this cycle of violence (13:24-30), every other Matthean parable that features slaves in either central or supporting roles describes the physical violation of at least some of those slaves (Matt. 18:23-35; 21:33-41; 22:1-10; 24:45-51; 25:14-30). Slaves are seized, imprisoned, treated with dishonor, beaten, cut in pieces, handed over to torturers, consigned to a place of "weeping and gnashing of teeth," killed, and stoned. This list of injuries to slaves' bodies is evidence of first-century familiarity with the travails of enslaved life.

Slaves in several of Matthew's parables command considerable wealth. Because of their access to wealth, many readers of Matthew have found it difficult to fit them into the category of slave. However, the more we know about slavery in the Roman Empire, the more credible this identification becomes. Some slaves in the Roman Empire rose to positions of considerable authority, influence, and even wealth. The best known of these powerful slaves were members of the family of Caesar. As personal attendants and financial agents, these slaves had unique access to the most powerful individuals in the empire. Free persons who sought access to those powerful individuals might strategically curry favor with well-placed slaves.

Because free persons relied on slaves to handle finances, many slaves enjoyed access to wealth. A few slaves accumulated personal funds that amounted to small fortunes. However, such slaves were still liable to whatever punishment an owner might choose to mete out. So, for example, Matthew recounts the parable of the unmerciful slave (18:23-35). A slave who belongs to a king owes the king ten thousand talents, a staggering sum. The magnitude of the debt suggests a slave who enjoys seemingly unlimited access to the king's coffers. The king is at first inclined to sell the slave and his family in order to recoup the debt but responds to the slave's plea for mercy and agrees to wait for payment. The slave turns around and imprisons a fellow slave who owes him a much smaller debt. When the king discovers the unmerciful slave's cruelty, he responds by handing him over to torturers.

Again, contemporary readers may take that as an exaggeration, but many of the punishments employed by ancient slaveholders qualified as torture under any definition. In some parts of the ancient Mediterranean world, slave owners hired public officials to discipline their slaves. An inscription from the Italian city of Puteoli detailed the job description of a *manceps*, which included the task of torturing and executing slaves on demand. The *manceps* supplied the equipment.[9] In this context the king's directive that his slave should be handed over to torturers hardly seems fanciful.

In the parable of the talents, the slaves are financial agents. The master entrusts them with his wealth—and keeps them in check with force (25:14-30; cf. Luke 19:11-27). The "wicked" third slave explains to his owner that he has buried his single talent because his master is a harsh man, whom he fears. The "good and faithful" slaves do not identify fear as a motivation.

Surely, however, they are aware that vulnerability to physical abuse is inherent in the situation of the slave. Classicist Richard Saller writes of Roman slavery, "The lot of bad slaves was to be beaten and that of good slaves was to internalize the constant threat of a beating."[10] Parables that conclude with wicked slaves enduring corporal punishment allude to the strongest incentive slaves had for loyalty to their owners: fear of disciplinary retribution.

In Roman law and practice, slaves lacked the ability to protect their own bodies. Although in many parables the abuse occurs as disciplinary action, slaves in several parables act violently toward fellow slaves. In the two Matthean parables where slaves are killed, the violent encounters take place outside the master's household, as slaves perform duties required of them. For example, in the parable of the vineyard, wicked tenants beat and then kill the slaves sent to collect rent (21:33-41; cf. Mark 12:1-12; Luke 20:9-19). The vineyard owner anticipates that the tenants will treat his son with greater respect. He understands that a son merits respect that is denied to slaves. His logic makes sense in a society structured by slaveholding.

In the opening of this chapter, I noted that, despite the familiarity of the parables, the slaves who populate the parables are somehow unfamiliar to readers today. One likely reason is that the King James Bible and other influential English-language translations render *doulos* as "servant" rather than "slave." My analysis of the parables suggests an additional reason for this lack of familiarity: for those unacquainted with some of the distinctive elements of Roman slavery, including the substantial wealth accumulated by a few slaves and the violence to which all slaves were vulnerable, the slave parables may seem fantastic. In addition, there may be a third reason why the slaves of the parables remain unfamiliar: quite simply, today's Christian readers of the Gospels are uncomfortable to confront the degree to which the parables rely on troubling assumptions about the relationships between slaves and slaveholders. To say that Jesus relies on the patterns of slaveholding in his parables does not mean Jesus therefore approves of those patterns of behavior. Nevertheless, he does not explicitly repudiate those behaviors.

As I argue in the next section, the gospel Jesus proclaims is incompatible with slaveholding values. To live out the gospel, then, we need to be honest about the ways in which our patterns of thinking are unwittingly complicit with a system in tension with the gospel. Readers of the Gospels come to recognize the disciplined flesh of parabolic slaves as an antitype, a model to avoid. Curiously, however, the Gospels feature another tortured body as a model to emulate: the battered and crucified body of Jesus. In a peculiar way the corporal punishment of disobedient slaves in the parables foreshadows the broken body of Jesus, ridiculed, beaten, and executed. The good news about Jesus and the good news he proclaims can strengthen us as we work to rectify the bad news in the world around us.

The Death of a Slave

One saying attributed to Jesus stands out for its implicit challenge to the ethos of slaveholding. According to the Gospel of Mark, Jesus instructs his close followers, "Whoever wishes to become great among you must be your servant, and whoever wishes to be first among you must be slave of all" (Mark 10:43-44; compare Matt. 20:26-27 and Luke 22:26).[11]

The Gospel of John does not include this saying, but an incident in John reflects a variant of the teaching. According to John, in the hours before Jesus' betrayal, he washed his disciples' feet and instructed them that they must likewise serve one another: "So if I, your Lord and Teacher, have washed your feet, you also ought to wash one another's feet. For I have set you an example, that you also should do as I have done to you" (John 13:14-15). Foot washing was a chore assigned to one of the least regarded slaves in a household, a role often played by women. The Fourth Gospel thus depicts a Jesus who defied the hierarchical and gender norms of his day. In this Johannine scene, Jesus embodies the part of the slave of all, a slave who desires "not to be served but to serve, and to give his life as a ransom for many" (Mark 10:45). John's inclusion of the scene testifies that early Christians associated Jesus with a challenge to the slaveholding ethos.

Jews and pagans in the ancient world sometimes styled themselves as "slaves of God" or "slaves of [some god]." A slave might boast that he or she was "slave of Caesar." Such appellations advanced the status of the person so-named. Not so with the designation "slave of all." The slaveholding ethos was predicated on control and honor. By calling on his followers, whether they were slaves, freedpersons, impoverished freeborn persons, or even members of slaveholding families, to become slaves to all, Jesus emptied that ethos of its power.

Early Christians struggled to live out the implications of this saying. So Paul wrote to the Galatians, "Become slaves to one another" (Gal. 5:13). But because the early Christian community did not forbid or place conditions on the baptism of slaveholders, the power of this mandate was, at best, limited. It is an interesting thought experiment to ponder how differently Christianity might have developed if early Christian communities had made freeing one's slaves a precondition of baptism.

From the first century to the twenty-first, the church has failed to live up to the radical demands of the gospel. The demands of the gospel are still radical. Directed toward slaveholders in the first century, directed toward CEOs in the twenty-first century, Jesus' words dare listeners: Be slaves to one another. Become the slave of all.

We should not approach this saying without awareness of its resonance over two thousand years of Christian history. Too often, these words have been beaten—metaphorically and often literally—into slaves, women, and other subordinates. As a result, many Christians today recoil from such imagery. For those who have fought to free themselves from internalized oppression, an insistence that slavery is a paradigm for discipleship is cringe-worthy. We must therefore recall that Jesus emptied of its force the mentality of slaveholding and thus the ethos of slavery.

In calling his followers to serve as slaves, as I have noted, Jesus refers to his own example: "For the Son of Man came not to be served but to serve, and to give his life as a ransom for many" (Mark 10:45). The image of the slave-Jesus whose self-giving death set an example for his followers was picked up in an early Christian hymn quoted by Paul in his letter to the Philippians (2:5-8):

> Let the same mind be in you that you have in
> Christ Jesus,
>> who, though he was in the form of God,
>>> did not regard equality with God
>>> as something to be exploited,

> but emptied himself,
>> taking the form of a slave,
>> being born in human likeness.
> And being found in human form,
>> he humbled himself
>> and became obedient to the point of death—
>> even death on a cross.

In coming to terms with Jesus' teachings on slavery, then, we recall not only his words but also his actions—indeed, according to the Philippians hymn, his very being. A community that conforms itself to him has no place for masters.

The Death of Slavery

So what, exactly, are we to make of widespread references to slaves in the sayings tradition?

Did Jesus endorse or enforce the norms of slavery? No. Unlike the early Christians who composed the letters of the deuteropauline tradition, Jesus did not teach, "Tell slaves to be submissive to their masters and to give satisfaction in every respect; they are not to talk back, not to pilfer, but to show complete and perfect fidelity" (Titus 2:9-10; compare Col. 3:22–4:1; Eph. 6:5-9; 1 Tim. 6:1-2). Although Jesus peppered his stories with images of battered slaves, he never taught, "Slaves, accept the authority of your masters with all deference, not only those who are kind and gentle but also those who are harsh. . . . If you endure pain when you are beaten for doing wrong, what credit is that? But if you endure when you do right and suffer for it, you have God's approval" (1 Peter 2:18-20).

Did Jesus urge an end to the system of slavery? No, but it's hard to see how he could effectively do so.

Perhaps more to the point, Jesus did not urge his followers who were slaves to resist or run away. Furthermore, we encounter no suggestion that he urged would-be followers who were slaveholders to free their slaves.

Rather, the sayings tradition suggests that slavery was prominent among the realities of everyday life that entered into Jesus' stories. This is not surprising, of course. Slavery was a significant factor in the world in which Jesus lived and in the communities that preserved and transformed the memory of Jesus and his words. Attention to the frequency and consistency of Jesus' references to the battered bodies of slaves should alert us to the persistent and intense violence of ancient slavery.

At the same time, awareness of the dishonor associated with slavery should bring us a fresh appreciation of the newness of Jesus' mandate to his followers to embrace the role of "slave of all." Jesus died an excruciating and humiliating death, the death of a slave. This death is a model for the disciple's life. Jesus does not condemn the institution of slavery. What he demands is something unexpected. He stipulates that his followers are to become a community of slaves serving one another.

How strange this mandate must have seemed in the first century. How strange it seems today.

2

The First Christian Slaveholders

The writings of Paul offer an ambivalent legacy for Christians struggling to come to terms with the impact of slavery on the emergence of Christianity. The apostle of freedom, Paul proclaimed that for those baptized in Christ "there is no longer Jew or Greek, there is no longer slave or free, there is no longer male and female" (Gal. 3:28; cf. 1 Cor. 12:13). Yet a number of letters attributed to Paul articulate household rules that include injunctions to slaves to obey their masters. In 1 Timothy slaves are even instructed to work extra hard for owners who are fellow Christians (6:2). Such household rules make it hard to imagine any sense in which early Christian communities transcended differences between slave and free.

Household codes mandating obedience for slaves appear in Colossians, Ephesians, 1 Timothy, and Titus. These epistles are often called "deuteropauline" because their authorship is disputed. New Testament scholars question whether these epistles were actually composed by Paul. But American Christians who debated slavery in the nineteenth century understood the apostle Paul to be the author, as do the majority of Christians today.

Although the common understanding is that the Pauline legacy includes mandates to slaves to submit to their masters, I will postpone to chapter 3 any discussion of the epistles whose Pauline authorship is disputed. The current chapter focuses on the place of slavery in the earliest churches, especially the churches that corresponded with Paul. It also focuses on Paul's theological perspectives on slavery and freedom.

Paul's own record on slavery has moral contradictions. Liberation is central to his proclamation of the gospel. At the same time, he relied on slaveholders to host church gatherings. We know the name of at least one of those slaveholders, Philemon. In reading Paul, we encounter the promise of the gospel to liberate. At the same time, we are confronted by the constraints under which the first Christian communities lived out that promise. Without denying the insidious impact of slavery on early Christian thought and practice, our challenge is to hear the good news at the heart of Paul's teaching.

Slavery and the Earliest Churches

According to Acts of the Apostles, Paul was not the first to baptize either slaves or slaveholders. Perhaps those baptisms took place as early as Pentecost. Acts pictures Peter quoting at length from the prophet Joel. Memorably, Peter proclaims:

> "Even upon my slaves, both men and women,
>   in those days I will pour out my Spirit;
>   and they shall prophesy." (Acts 2:18)

"Those who welcomed his message were baptized," we're told, "and that day about three thousand persons were added" (Acts 2:41). Were slaves among the newly baptized? Luke, the author of Acts of the Apostles, does not say so. Still, it's easy to imagine that some slaves who mingled in that Pentecost crowd welcomed the good news.

According to Luke's idealized portrait, the very young Jerusalem church enjoyed a community of goods. Members of the Jerusalem church sold their land and houses in order to provide for the community (Acts 4:32-37; cf. 2:43-47). By creating this idealized portrait, Luke implies that the early converts included at least a few propertied individuals. Such individuals might be expected to own a slave or two, or more. Luke's brief, evocative references to a utopian community of goods do not touch on the question of the role of slaves, freed slaves, or slaveholders in that community.

As soon as Luke moves away from his idyllic portrayal of the primitive community of goods, he depicts both Jewish and Gentile slaveholders as members of the church. Cornelius, for example, was a Gentile who feared the God of Israel. A centurion who prayed and gave alms, Cornelius was told in a vision to send for Peter. He sent two of his slaves along with a soldier to find Peter. Peter had also had a vision. He therefore agreed to accompany the enslaved emissaries and the soldier. Cornelius described his visionary experience. Peter then witnessed the Holy Spirit descend on the kinfolk and friends Cornelius had assembled—a cohort that presumably included Cornelius's household slaves. Peter agreed to baptize the assembly (Acts 10). From the outset, suggests Acts of the Apostles, slaveholders were crucial to the expansion of the gospel message into Gentile communities.

In Mary of Jerusalem, Acts portrays a slaveholder whose house was a well-known gathering place for members of the Way. When Peter was miraculously delivered from prison he quickly found his way there. A prayer gathering was in progress. When Peter knocked at the gate, a slave named Rhoda greeted him (11:12-16). Acts creates the impression that both Mary and Rhoda, slaveholder and slave, were present at the prayer gathering.

The brief vignette of Mary and Rhoda brings home several points about the place of slavery in the earliest churches. First, women as well as men could be slaveholders, and women as well as men could be enslaved. Second, in order for the movement to expand, believers had to find meeting places. Houses large enough to accommodate prayer meetings were likely to number slaves among members of the household. Third, slaveholders and slaves could belong to the same congregation. Recognition that slaveholders worshipped alongside their own slaves raises the question of whether baptism transformed relations between owners and their human property. We turn to the letters of Paul with this question in mind.

The Slaveholder Philemon and the Church in His House

It seems that Paul's brief letter to Philemon should help us consider the impact of baptism on relations between a slaveholder and his or her slave. In some ways it does, yet Philemon is also a frustrating source, resisting the questions we pose. In it Paul addressed the slaveholder Philemon, whom he called a "dear friend and co-worker" Along with Philemon, Paul also addressed "Apphia the sister" and "Archippus the fellow soldier" (v. 1). After naming these three individuals, Paul addressed the church that met in Philemon's house. The letter would have been read aloud to the assembly of the baptized that convened in Philemon's house.

Paul wrote from prison. The emissary carrying the letter was Onesimus, a slave belonging to Philemon. The letter revolves around Onesimus's relationships with Paul and Philemon. While in prison, Paul wrote, he became Onesimus's father (v. 10), implying that he baptized Onesimus. As a result Onesimus was returning to Philemon "no longer as a slave but more than a slave, a beloved brother—especially to me but how much more to you, both in the flesh and in the Lord" (v. 16). But there seems to have been some past trouble between Philemon and Onesimus. Paul wrote, "If he [Onesimus] has wronged you in any way, or owes you anything, charge that to my account" (v. 18). The original recipients of the letter knew the history of that interpersonal difficulty. Modern readers do not.

The letter is brief, even cryptic. Our basic questions remain unanswered. Why was Onesimus with Paul in prison? Traditionally, it was understood that Onesimus had run away from Philemon. A runaway Onesimus would account for Philemon's grievance. Alternatively, perhaps Philemon had sent Onesimus to assist Paul in prison; prisoners typically relied on outside networks for food and other sustenance. If Philemon had sent Onesimus to Paul, there would have been some other cause for grievance. Perhaps Onesimus stole money or goods from Philemon. We do not know.[1]

What did Paul expect from Philemon? Did he want Onesimus to return to assist him in prison, as suggested by his statement that "I wanted to keep him with me, so that he might be of service to me in your place during my imprisonment for the gospel; but I preferred to do nothing without your consent, in order that your good deed might be voluntary and not something forced"

(v. 13)? When Paul wrote that he knew Philemon would "do even more than I say" (v. 21), did he expect the slaveholder to free the baptized slave?

At the heart of this brief letter is Paul's expectation regarding the slaveholder Philemon's treatment of his slave Onesimus—yet we cannot identify that expectation with certainty. As I said at the outset of this discussion, Philemon is a frustrating source! Let us therefore consider another approach to the letter, an approach that focuses not on what Paul asked but on how he phrased his request—or, more accurately, his demand.[2]

In crafting his charge to Philemon, Paul relied heavily on family imagery. Church members who gathered in Philemon's house to hear the letter read aloud would have had different associations with that imagery than twenty-first-century readers. On a very basic level, neither Greek nor Latin had an exact equivalent for the English word *family*. The household unit was not defined by the nuclear family. Slaves were considered members of the household—members who were perpetually dependent and subordinate.

Today, family imagery is associated with intimacy and affection. In antiquity, too, many family bonds were intimate bonds of love. Maternal love was often idealized, for example. Children were expected to return that love.

At the same time, the family or household was understood as an economic unit under the authority of the head of the household. The Latin term *paterfamilias* captured that sense of authority. The *paterfamilias* might love his wife and his children, yet the term was more associated with hierarchical authority than with warm, fuzzy feelings. The authority of the *paterfamilias* extended not only to his wife and children. His authority also extended to other household dependents and to household slaves.

We are likely to hear Paul's declaration that he had become Onesimus's father (v. 10) as a statement of affection. It is that, but it is more as well. Paul's declaration that he had become Onesimus's father was a declaration of authority. By asserting his own paternal authority over "his child" Onesimus, Paul subtly displaced the authority of Philemon as head of household.

Not only did Paul claim to displace Philemon as Onesimus's "father," he additionally positioned Philemon and Onesimus as brothers. Paul directed Philemon to receive Onesimus "no longer as a slave but more than a slave, a beloved brother—especially to me but how much more to you, both in the flesh and in the Lord" (v. 16). In the new family of the church, Philemon and Onesimus, slaveholder and slave, were recast as brothers.

Paul also addressed Philemon as his "brother" (vv. 7, 20). On one level, Paul, Philemon, and Onesimus were beloved brothers through baptism. At the same time, however, Paul insisted on his authority over both Philemon and Onesimus. Paul declared his authority not only through his declaration that he was Onesimus's father but also by his reminder that Philemon owed Paul his very self. Over both Onesimus and Philemon, Paul thus exercised the authority of the *paterfamilias*. Even though Paul understood that the nature of Philemon's authority over Onesimus had been redefined, Onesimus was not a free agent. He was now under a different authority, the authority of his "father," Paul.

At stake is the question of whether baptism altered the dynamics of household relations between slaveholder and slave. Onesimus legally remained Philemon's property. He was also Philemon's brother "in the flesh and in the Lord" (v. 16). How did this newly forged fraternity affect their day-to-day lives? Would Philemon give orders to a brother who, legally, was still his property? Would Onesimus feel compelled to obey Philemon, his legal owner? Or would he be emboldened to challenge Philemon, whom he could now call brother?

Throughout his letters, Paul rendered opinions about the conduct of Christian life. How would those instructions have been heard in households where both slaveholder and slave were baptized?[3] For example, Paul instructed the Galatian Christians that through love they should be slaves to one another (5:13). In chapter 1, I presented this teaching as central to the gospel. On a practical level, however, how would this mandate work in a slaveholding Christian household? Paul wrote the Galatians that, empowered by the Spirit, they should take the initiative to correct fellow members of the church who transgressed. Such corrections should transpire in the spirit of gentleness (6:1). But we can imagine that a slave might instead be filled with the spirit of timidity. To suppose that the fact of legal slavery would not affect the behavior of enslaved Christians toward their Christian owners strains the imagination.

Paul expected Philemon to welcome Onesimus as a brother. At the same time he hesitated to spell out the implications of this brotherhood. Like many contemporary readers, I am unsure what Paul expected from Philemon. The ambiguity of the epistle may be deliberate. Without telling Philemon what to do, Paul invited Philemon to decide on his own course of action, a course of action to be determined by love (v. 9). In many other situations Paul outlined his understanding of demands of love. He did not do so when writing the slaveholder Philemon. Perhaps as he wrote his letter to Philemon, Paul remained uncertain about the claims of the gospel, the claims of love, in a situation where one brother claimed ownership of another brother.[4]

Baptized into One Body

In Galatians, Paul promises that among the baptized there is no longer "Jew or Greek, slave or free, male and female" (3:28). In 1 Corinthians, Paul proclaims, "For in the one Spirit we were all baptized into one body—Jews or Greeks, slaves or free—and we were all made to drink of one Spirit" (12:13).

Do these two passages say the same thing about baptism and slavery? Unlike Galatians, 1 Corinthians does not suggest that divisions between slave and free are obsolete among the baptized. Rather, 1 Corinthians proclaims that both slave and free are incorporated into the body of Christ. Does membership in that body overcome distinctions between slaves and freepersons? Perhaps we should divide that question in two. First, as the community lived out the promise of baptism, did they transcend differences between enslaved members and free members? Second, even if they did not, did Paul believe they should?

In Corinth, both slaves and freepersons were among the baptized. Paul wrote, "Consider your own call, brothers and sisters: not many of you were wise by human standards, not many were powerful, not many were of noble birth" (1 Cor. 1:26). The Corinthian church had many members who were humble, even "low and despised" (1:28). While members of higher social status were in a minority, they were present in the church.

Paul learned about the doings of the Corinthian Christians from "Chloe's people" (1:11). "Chloe's people" were probably household slaves belonging to the otherwise unknown Chloe. We may speculate that, like her slaves, Chloe was a member of the church. Perhaps the Corinthian church even met in her home. If not, the church almost certainly met in the home of another baptized slaveholder.

When the Corinthian church gathered to worship, they sang hymns, shared prophecies, spoke in tongues, and taught one another (14:26). They also shared a meal, the Lord's Supper. We do not know who served the meal. If a slave ordinarily served a household meal, would he or she recline when the meal commemorated the Lord's Supper? If so, who would serve?

Paul complained that the community's commemorations of the Lord's Supper did not deserve that name: "When you come together, it is not really to eat the Lord's supper. For when the time comes to eat, each of you goes ahead with our own supper, and one goes hungry and another becomes drunk" (11:20-21). A common interpretation of this passage suggests that the divisions apparent at the Lord's Supper were rooted in distinctions of wealth. Perhaps those who were wealthier were served finer fare, a common practice at ancient dinner parties. Paul wrote, "When you come together to eat, wait for one another" (11:33). Those first to the table were likely individuals whose lives were marked by leisure. Those late to the table were likely laborers, and among them, slaves.

In the context of the Lord's Supper, then, Paul believed that the Corinthian Christian community had not succeeded in overcoming status distinctions. We are confronted by the possibility that, even when gathering for worship, baptism into one body did not effectively erase distinctions between slaves and free persons. Paul urged the Corinthians to reorganize their community life so that those distinctions would not be divisive.

Let us consider the immediate context of Paul's proclamation that "in the one Spirit we were all baptized
into one body—Jews or Greeks, slaves or free" (12:13).
Paul reminded his readers of their baptism in the midst
of his discussion of the gifts of the Spirit—gifts such
as healing, prophesying, and teaching. Paul urged the
community honor all the gifts of its members. After all,
a body requires feet as well as hands, a nose as well as
ears. Extending his metaphor of the body, Paul pointed
out that "less respectable members" of the body (for
example, sexual organs) were treated with respect—that
is, by being covered to protect the body's honor. Even
so, Paul urged the Corinthians, they should avoid the
trap of singling out some church members as honorable.
Distinctions between honor and dishonor mattered in
the world, but they should not divide church members.
Instead, Paul urged the Corinthians to consider the good
of the community. The community required the Spirit-
endowed contributions of all participants.

Sociologically, it is difficult to map Paul's body
metaphor onto specific relations within the Corinthian
community. Paul wanted the Corinthian Christians to
appreciate that the showier gifts of the Spirit—speaking
in tongues, for example—were not relevant for build-
ing up the community. That humblest of spiritual gifts,
self-giving love, was most important of all. It is possible
that by showy displays of spiritual power, slaves and
other marginalized persons asserted authority within
the community. It is also possible that the wealthier
members of the congregation were more likely to boast
of such gifts. Perhaps this is why Paul's reflection on
spiritual gifts follows his criticism of the Corinthian
Christians for their behavior in conducting the Lord's
Supper. On this interpretation, by reminding the Corinthians to respect "the inferior member," Paul advocated

respect for less advantaged members of the community, including enslaved members.

By situating his observation that "we were all baptized into one body—Jews or Greeks, slaves or free" in the context of his wider discussion of the gifts of the Spirit, Paul attempted to minimize the significance of legal status distinctions within the Christian community. This is not a description of the way things were in the Corinthian community but a statement of how things ought to be. On Paul's view the church should transcend social distinctions, including distinctions between slave and free.

Yet Paul did not develop an antislavery agenda. Paul's pronounced lack of urgency regarding legal bondage makes it difficult for many of today's Christians to fully trust his commitment to the freedom promised by the gospel. To put it bluntly, for many contemporary Christians—and still more non-Christians—Paul's tolerance of slaveholding within the church undermines his moral authority. If, as I have argued, transcending distinctions between slave and free was an ideal for Paul, what held him back from pushing this agenda in the churches he founded?

Just the Way You Are

For a better understanding of Paul's lack of urgency regarding the status of slaves and slaveholders in the community, we can find some clues in 1 Corinthians 7. First, Paul held that the legal conditions of freedom or slavery were relative. Second, he believed that the familiar world was already fading from view. As a result the structures of society were ultimately doomed. It will be helpful for us to consider his remarks on slavery in the context of the chapter as a whole.

This chapter of 1 Corinthians focuses on marriage between Christians. Paul wrote in response to questions posed by the Corinthians. He advised the married to remain married. He advised the unmarried that it was better to remain unmarried. Among other reasons, he noted that single women and men were better able to concentrate on "the affairs of the Lord" (7:32, 34). Married women and men were inevitably distracted by "the affairs of the world" (vv. 33, 34) and by trying to please their spouses.

Paul did not represent his advice as law. Unmarried persons who burned with unsatisfied passion—surely an enormous distraction!—would do better to satisfy their passions within marriage (v. 9). To the extent possible, however, Paul encouraged the Corinthians, "Let each of you remain in the condition in which you were called" (v. 20).

In the course of presenting his advice about whether or not to marry (or to stay married), Paul advised the still recently baptized Corinthians to accept other conditions of their lives. Those who were not circumcised should not seek circumcision. But by no means should the circumcised attempt to remove the marks of circumcision, as was sometimes done. Instead, Paul told the Corinthians, "Circumcision is nothing, and uncircumcision is nothing; but obeying the commands of God is everything" (v. 19).

Paul's advice on circumcision seems commonsensical today. More confusing, and problematic, is what he wrote in 1 Corinthians 7 about slavery. "Were you a slave when called?" Paul wrote. "Don't be concerned about it" (v. 21). Translators are sharply divided about what Paul intends to say in the continuation of this advice. Paul explicitly addresses slaves who have a chance to be manumitted—but what does he mean?

The New Revised Standard Version translates Paul's elliptical wording as advice that slaves should decline offers of manumission. In the words of the NRSV, Paul advises, "Make use of your present condition now more than ever" (v. 21). In a groundbreaking work on manumission in early Christianity, however, New Testament scholar J. Albert Harrill argues persuasively that the passage should instead be translated as encouragement to slaves to seize their chances for manumission. How does this affect the logic of Paul's argument in 1 Corinthians 7?

As I have noted, 1 Corinthians 7 articulates a general principle for Christian life. Each believer should remain content with the state in which he or she was called. Throughout chapter 7, however, Paul offered exceptions to this rule. Although he wrote that spouses should be content to remain married, he established guidelines for spouses seeking separation (v. 11). He encouraged those who were single to be content with that status, but stated that they did not sin if they chose to marry (v. 28). Similarly, after telling slaves not to be disturbed by their bondage, Paul then offered an exception: "If you can indeed become free, seize [the opportunity]" (v. 21).

Paul's advice to seize an opportunity for manumission was not abolitionist. He recognized the relative desirability of being free. No one in antiquity would have disagreed. Most who were born in slavery died in slavery, but manumission was common throughout the Roman Empire. Many slaves were motivated by the hope that obedience and hard work would result in their eventual freedom. Some slaves realized this dream. More did not. Not surprisingly, then, Paul advised enslaved Christians: If you have a chance to be free, go for it.

Paul's views on freedom and slavery tempered his concern with slavery in the Christian community. For Paul both freedom and slavery were relative states. Everyone was in bondage to some force, but only those who were in Christ could be said to be free. Paul wrote, "For whoever was called in the Lord as a slave is a freed person belonging to the Lord, just as whoever was free when called is a slave of Christ" (v. 22). A baptized slave was free in the ways that Paul believed to matter. Recall Paul's words to Philemon: Onesimus returned to Philemon "no longer as a slave, but more than a slave, a beloved brother" (Phlm. 16).

Paul associated Christian freedom with voluntary submission—to Christ and to other members of the church (compare Gal. 5:13). Paul believed that enslaved Christians enjoyed Christian freedom. He believed that all Christians, slave and free, shared in a loving mutual enslavement. As a result he did not treat release from legal slavery as an urgent priority.

Through the ages many Christian readers have been persuaded by Paul's bid to downplay the significance of enslavement. On this view, when a slave is baptized, he or she becomes "a freedperson belonging to Christ." Given the surpassing value of Christian freedom, many well-meaning Christians have reasoned, what ultimate harm can there be in the state of enslavement?

A related view was held in Paul's day by philosophers known as Stoics. Stoics believed that the situation of a slave was no different from the situation of a free person in the only respect they thought mattered: the freedom of judgment and moral decision making. There was no essential distinction between slave and free. A proud freeborn person could nonetheless be a slave to passions. A slave might thus be more truly free than the emperor.

The view that a person's legal status as slave does not destroy his or her essential freedom, a view as much Stoic as Christian, is in some ways attractive. It can be of great comfort to slaves and prisoners. This Stoic view, however, disguises the real harm of slavery. This harm is brought into sharp relief if we think about enslaved children or the sexual exploitation of slaves.

Some adults have the fortitude to behave freely though legally bound. Such fortitude is praiseworthy. But we can imagine that a child raised as a slave would routinely, if not inevitably, internalize a sense of inferiority. In his "Letter from Birmingham Jail," Dr. Martin Luther King Jr. poignantly wrote about the challenges of raising children under Jim Crow laws. In his words, it became impossible to wait for gradual change "as you seek to explain to your six-year-old daughter why she can't go to the public amusement park that has just been advertised on television, and see tears welling up in her eyes when she is told that Funtown is closed to colored children, and see ominous clouds of inferiority beginning to form in her little mental sky."[5] Although there is no reason to think anyone in the first century held the views on individual human rights that were held by King in the mid-twentieth century, King's "Letter from Birmingham Jail" invites reflection on the enduring damage of growing up under exploitative circumstances. If we think about the children of enslaved Corinthian Christians, we are likely to question Paul's view of slavery as only a relative liability.

Paul did not address the sexual exploitation that was endemic to all forms of ancient slavery. If he had, perhaps he would have been more concerned about the impact of slavery on the baptized. Paul argued strongly in 1 Cor. 6:12-20 that sexual relations could not be morally neutral. This reasoning would have posed problems for many slaves who desired new life in Christ. Throughout the Roman world, enslaved women, girls, and boys were the sexual property of their owners. This was true in both Gentile and Jewish communities.

We do not know how Paul responded to the sexual use of slaves. Could Paul have accepted that sexual couplings between (male) slaveholders and their (female) slaves were simply a fact of life? If not, how would he have advised slaves whose owners insisted on sexual favors? In at least this one domain, the fact of slavery would have complicated Paul's expectation that slave status should have no impact on Christian life. Paul taught that legal slavery was no impediment to Christian freedom. Was that true for a newly baptized slave whose master pressed her for sexual favors he perceived as his due?

Paul was hardly the only moralist, ancient or modern, to be more attuned to the moral questions faced by free adult men than the moral questions faced by vulnerable dependents. One has only to think of the tragic tendency of the Roman Catholic Church to respond to pedophilia as a clerical weakness rather than a crime against a child. Yet this problem is hardly confined to Catholicism. Most churches, in fact, remain reluctant to preach against incest and other forms of child abuse. Such preaching might alienate adult churchgoers who are financial patrons. In chapter 4, I will argue that attention to Christian acquiescence in the sexual use of slaves can help us to unlearn harmful attitudes that persist into the present.

Paul's lack of urgency in addressing the situation of slavery implies a reluctance or inability to recognize the moral harm of slavery to the slave. That harm comes into sharp relief if we think about enslaved children or about the sexual vulnerabilities of slaves. However,

Paul's lack of concern for the damages of slavery—and thus for the moral wrong of slaveholding—was additionally influenced by his conviction that the end was near. To understand more fully why Paul did not care about reforming the structures of his day, it will be helpful to return to his arguments about marriage in 1 Corinthians 7.

For much of Christian history, children have been central to teachings about the purpose of marriage. In an entire chapter devoted to marriage, however, Paul said remarkably little about children. He referred to children only to back up his contention that one unbelieving spouse "makes holy" the other. "Otherwise," Paul wrote, "your children would be unclean, but as it is, they are holy" (7:14).

Why didn't Paul care about the next generation of Christians? He didn't expect there to be one. He expected the end of the world to come in his lifetime. In 1 Thessalonians he wrote of the return of Jesus:

> For the Lord himself, with a cry of command, with the archangel's call and with the sound of God's trumpet, will descend from heaven, and the dead in Christ will rise first. Then we who are alive, who are left, will be caught up in the clouds together with them to meet the Lord in the air; and so we will be with the Lord forever. (4:16-17)

In other writings Paul expressed his apocalyptic understanding differently. Paul understood the crucifixion of Jesus to mark a turning point in the ages. It brought an end to "the present evil age" (Gal. 1:3). Not surprisingly, Paul's understanding of the turn of the ages (the end of one age and the beginnings of another) informed his marital advice in 1 Corinthians 7: "I mean, . . . the appointed time has grown short; from now on, let even those who have wives be as though they had none" (v. 29). The cares of marriage were among the cares of the world, a world that no longer much mattered, on Paul's view: "For the present form of this world is passing away" (v. 31).

Paul perceived that he was at the turn of the ages. He valued freedom over slavery, but he did not think human relations would be defined by slavery in the age to come. He felt little motivation to reform the structures of a world that was passing away. Even so, we should recall that in other contexts, Paul expressed fierce concern about attachment to practices he associated with a world passing away. One need think only of his ire over Gentile Christians seeking circumcision in Galatia, an ire never roused by slavery.

In 1 Corinthians 7, Paul urged Christians not to be distracted by the petty affairs of a dying world, and to concentrate instead on the affairs of the Lord. From a latter-day perspective, we may instead perceive that Paul, distracted by the end times, failed to recognize the full implications of the gospel of freedom he preached. Paul never stated that he saw slaveholding as incompatible with the gospel. He believed that within the church community, divisions between slave and free should be immaterial. We may nonetheless infer that Paul was insensitive to the actual impact of slavery within the community of believers.

The Gospel of Freedom

I began this chapter with Paul's haunting declaration in Galatians that status distinctions are obsolete among the baptized: "There is no longer Jew or Greek, there is no longer slave or free, there is no longer male and female; for all of you are one in Christ Jesus" (3:28). Yet as we have seen, Christians did not live up to the promise of these words. Churches did not require manumission of slaves as a prerequisite for baptism. Even within the community, status distinctions based on gender and on identity as slave or free persisted.

Although the formula repeated by Paul proclaimed "there is no longer male and female," in practice he insisted on gender hierarchy. In 1 Corinthians 11, for example, he weighed the question of whether women should cover their heads when they prayed or prophesied (11:2-16). The discussion assumes that distinctions between male and female endure. Man may be the reflection of God, yet woman is the reflection of man (v. 7).[6]

In his epistle to the Galatians, Paul did not develop his thoughts on relations among baptized men and women. Gender is at most a peripheral concern in Galatians. Freedom, however, is central. According to Paul, life apart from Christ is lived as bondage (see 4:1-7). Through his death, Christ has freed us from "the present evil age" (1:4).

For Paul the good news has to do with our liberation by Christ. He insists on the importance of living into this freedom: "For freedom Christ has set us free. Stand firm, therefore, and do not submit again to a yoke of slavery" (5:1). Thus, although Paul does not develop in Galatians any thoughts on relations between baptized slaves and their baptized owners, it is impossible to read the letter without meditating on the centrality of freedom to the Christian life.

I find it curious that in developing his arguments about Christian freedom, Paul relied on metaphors that evoked the realities of slavery in the Roman world. Although Paul didn't evince unease about Christians who were slaves, his rhetoric was haunted by the

liabilities of slave status. Telling the Galatians that they
had been adopted as God's own children, he contrasted
their new identity with the lot of slaves, who were shut
out of inheritance (4:1-7). It seems that Paul was thinking of Roman law on slaves, sons, and inheritance.[7]

In a more extended metaphor, Paul relied on the
story of Sarah and Hagar as the basis of an allegori-
cal comparison between the freedom of the Galatian
church and the bondage of the Jerusalem church (4:21-
31). According to Genesis, Abraham's barren wife Sarah
gave her slave Hagar to her husband so that he could
father children. When Sarah at last gave birth to Isaac,
Hagar and her son Ishmael were expelled to the wilder-
ness (Gen. 16:1-16; 21:1-21). I take Hagar to exemplify
the vulnerabilities of ancient slaves to sexual exploitation and to brutality.

I will not trace Paul's complicated argument in Gal.
4:21-31.[8] What is relevant for our discussion is that,
in developing his argument about Christian freedom,
Paul relied on an allegory that underscored the liabilities of slave status. Paul didn't worry about the impact
of enslavement on members of his community. His lan-
guage was nonetheless haunted by the everyday ugli-
ness of slavery.

Paul summed up his understanding of Christian
freedom this way: "For you were called to freedom,
brothers and sisters; only do not use your freedom as
an opportunity for the flesh, but through love become
slaves to one another" (5:13). For Paul, Christian freedom doesn't mean that anything goes. Although Paul's
warning against freedom as "an opportunity for the
flesh" encompassed fornication and lust, his list of
the "works of the flesh" focused on divisive behavior:
"enmities, strife, jealousy, anger, quarrels, dissensions,
factions, envy" (5:20-21).

For Paul, the antidote to divisive behavior was clear. "Through love become slaves to one another." Paul formulated his understanding of Christian freedom in words that echoed Jesus' teaching that his followers were called to act as slaves. Once again we look in vain for a clear mandate to reject the practice of slave-holding. Instead we are told that life in Christ requires mutual submission—a dictate ultimately at odds with Roman notions of honor and other values associated with the institution of slavery. It is a dictate equally at odds with the consumerist and individualist values that suffuse contemporary life.

Slaves like Us

In several letters Paul styled himself a slave. In 1 Corinthians, Paul wrote, "For though I am free with respect to all, I have made myself a slave to all, so that I might win more of them" (9:19). Elsewhere Paul called himself a slave of Christ (Gal. 1:10; Rom. 1:1; Phil. 1:1). Some biblical scholars suggest that Paul used this title to elevate his own status in the community.[9] I understand the phrase differently.

One of the places where Paul refers to himself as a "slave of Christ" is the opening of Philippians. In that same letter Paul evokes the image of Jesus as slave. In chapter 1, we have already discussed the hymn quoted in Philippians 2:

> [Christ Jesus], though he was in the form of God,
>> did not regard equality with God
>> as something to be exploited,
> but emptied himself,
>> taking the form of a slave,
>> being born in human likeness. (vv. 6-7)

In the context of the Philippians hymn, Jesus' adoption of the identity of slave is seen as a self-humbling, self-emptying gesture that led to his humiliating death on the cross. In Galatians, another letter where Paul called himself slave of Christ (1:10), Paul claimed that it was no longer Paul who lived. Rather, the crucified—and thus servile—Christ lived in him (2:20). In this spirit, Paul understood himself as "slave of Christ."

If we approach Paul with the expectation that he will share our repugnance for the social institution of slavery, we will be disappointed.[10] It is important not to gloss over that disappointment. Paul seems to have been indifferent to the circumstances of church members who were slaves (and to the circumstances of prostituted slaves who might have wanted to join the church). In other contexts he was often blunt in his expression of disapproval, but he never cited slaveholding as a moral wrong.

We cannot judge the first century by the standards of the twenty-first. Nonetheless, we should be aware of the traces of such attitudes in our own day. Now that our society outlaws slavery, it is easy to identify slaveholding as evil, yet we continue to be slow to name the harmful behaviors of powerful interests as moral wrongs.

Although Paul did not forbid Christians to be slaveholders, he nonetheless challenged slaveholding values, a challenge that resonates today. As we have seen, Paul understood Christian freedom as mutual submission: "Through love become slaves to one another" (Gal. 5:13). In calling himself slave of Christ, Paul held himself up as an exemplar of such peculiar freedom.

3

Slaves in the Household
of God

During the first century of Christian life, we find very few references to Jesus Christ or to Christianity in pagan sources. One of those rare references also supplies a nugget of evidence about slave involvement in the church.

Pliny the Younger served as governor in a territory in Asia Minor, present-day Turkey. Sometime around 112 C.E., Pliny wrote the emperor Trajan to ask whether there was an imperial policy on how to treat accusations against Christians. He explained that if the accused were willing to offer suitable sacrifices to the emperor and to curse Christ, he let them go. He thus released those who admitted they had been Christians but were willing to recant. Those who would not curse Christ were found guilty. They were executed. Pliny explained that he wanted to know more about Christianity. He wrote, "I judged it so much the more necessary to extract the real truth, with the assistance of torture, from two female slaves, who were styled deaconesses [or ministers], but I could discover nothing more than depraved and excessive superstition."[1]

In the discussion of Jesus' parables in chapter 1, I noted that it was common for the corporal punishment of slaves to qualify as torture. Citizens were protected from many forms of physical abuse (although those protections had begun to diminish by the second century). Indeed, one of the chief distinctions between slave and free was the vulnerability of slaves to torture and other forms of violence. A slave's testimony in a trial was customarily rendered under torture. Pliny probably sought out slave informants precisely because they could be tortured. He may also have focused on the two enslaved women because he perceived them to be leaders in their church. We don't know what role the women played in their communities, but Pliny identifies them as ministers.

Like other writings from the ancient Mediterranean, Christian sources are heavily weighted toward the perspectives of freeborn men. There are exceptions. For example, *The Shepherd of Hermas* dates from the early to mid-second century. It was well known and influential among Christians of the second and third centuries. Hermas states that he had been raised as a slave. He begins the work, "He who raised me sold me to a certain Rhoda at Rome."[2] The authors of some other early Christian works may have been freedpersons or slaves, but we cannot positively identify them as such.

Every generation of Christians included slaves, yet our evidence about those slaves is at best fragmentary. How eager we would be to read a letter between the two women tortured by Pliny!

This chapter focuses on moral questions raised by Christian writings in the generations after Paul. I begin with Pliny's reference to enslaved women ministers for a simple reason. Although enslaved Christians did not leave a written record, they nonetheless strengthened early communities. They were present at gatherings for worship—singing hymns, praying, and living out the good news. As we study the writings of freeborn men, we should consider how different our understanding of early Christian thought might be if we had documentary access to the perspectives of enslaved Christians.

The Gospel: What's the Difference?

The teachings of Jesus and Paul are crucial to Christians struggling to make sense of the legacy of slavery and early Christianity. I have therefore explored those teachings in the first half of this book. In the second half, I consider the impact of those teachings over the first centuries of the Church. I am concerned with a number of questions.

Some of the questions have to do with Christian practice. One question I have already raised is whether baptism made any difference in relations between slave and slaveholder. What did Christians teach about the obligations of slaveholders and of slaves? Do we have any reason to believe that Christian slaveholders could be distinguished from Jewish or pagan slaveholders on the basis of their treatment of slaves? Is there reason to think slaves changed their attitudes or behavior when they became Christians?

Other questions are theological. Regardless of the behavior of Christian slaves and Christian slaveholders, did the relations of slavery trouble Christian thinkers? Did *any* Christians find slavery to be incompatible with the gospel? How did the church reconcile teachings on human personhood with the subjugation inherent in slavery?

Answers to these questions are unsettling. In many ways, Christian teachings actually reinforced the power of the slaveholder, even as they affirmed the dignity of slaves in God's eyes. However, we also find scattered suggestions that a few Christians began to question the rightness of slaveholding. Examples of such moral insight and courage may hearten those who struggle for justice today.

Slavery was so basic a structure in the ancient world that challenging it might have seemed as odd as asking why water was wet or ice cold. Rather than wondering why it took so long for ancient Christians to recognize slavery as incompatible with the gospel, Christians today might better ask what contemporary structures that we take for granted are in fact inconsistent with the good news we proclaim.

Household Codes

Several Christian writings feature codes of household management. These codes prescribe behavior for husbands, wives, children, slaves, and slaveholders. Although these codes cannot tell us how slaves or slaveholders actually behaved, they lay out moral norms for believing communities. Household codes specifying expectations for slaves—and, in some cases, slaveholders—appear in Colossians, Ephesians, 1 Timothy, and Titus, all of which are attributed to Paul. First Peter offers parallel yet distinctive advice to slaves. Household codes also appear in the *Didache*, in circulation by the end of the first century, and the *Epistle of Barnabas*, which was in circulation several decades later.

New Testament commentaries sometimes suggest that the household codes were morally innovative because they addressed slaves as well as slaveholders. On this view the delivery of moral instruction to slaves is a liberating recognition of their moral autonomy. However, the household codes were not innovative in this respect. One parallel can be found in Roman manuals for estate management, which gear some of their advice directly to slaves.[3] Slaves in Christian household codes were told to subordinate their wills to the wills of their masters—hardly recognition of moral independence.

Colossians and Ephesians

The earliest Christian sources to include household codes are Colossians and Ephesians. Like most New Testament scholars, I am convinced that Paul was not the author of these works. However, no consensus on authorship exists. Even those who argue against Pauline authorship concede that the works date to shortly after the time of Paul or perhaps were written by one of Paul's coworkers.

Like Galatians, Colossians promises that among those brought to new life in Christ, "there is no longer Greek and Jew, circumcised and uncircumcised, barbarian, Scythian, slave and free; but Christ is all and in all!" (3:11). Despite this proclamation, Colossians underscores conventional expectations regarding the behavior of slaves:

> Slaves, obey your earthly masters [*kyrioi*, lords] in everything, not only while being watched and in order to please them, but wholeheartedly, fearing the Lord [*Kyrios*]. Whatever your task, put yourselves into it, as done for the Lord [*Kyrios*] and not for your masters [*kyrioi*], since you know that from the Lord [*Kyrios*] you will receive the inheritance as your reward; you are slaves of the Lord [*Kyrios*] Christ. (Col. 3:22-25)

As we saw in our discussion of Jesus' parables in chapter 1, fear supplied powerful motivation for slaves to obey their owners. In Colossians we find an intensification of that motivation. Slaves should fear not only their masters (*kyrioi*), they should also fear punishment by the Lord (*Kyrios*) Christ. In the words of New Testament scholar John Barclay, the household code in Colossians "comes extremely close to sanctioning the present hierarchical structures as if they were supervised and supported by the ultimate master, Christ."[4]

The abolition of cultic distinctions between slaves and slaveholders proclaimed a few verses earlier does not transform relations between slave and slaveholder. Colossians devotes more time to dictating behavior to slaves than to instructing wives, husbands, or children. Could this be a reaction against slaves who took literally the baptismal affirmation that distinctions between slave and free had been overcome?

Instructions to slaveholders in Colossians are comparably brief: "Masters [*kyrioi*], treat your slaves justly and fairly, for you know that you also have a Master [or Lord, *Kyrios*] in heaven" (4:1 NRSV). It may come as a relief to learn that Christian slaveholders were instructed to treat slaves "justly and fairly." However, such advice did not distinguish Christian from pagan moralists, who also urged moderate treatment of slaves. Many slaves were subjected to excessive and cruel treatment, yet one would be hard-pressed to find ancient writings that praised cruelty. It was also widely understood that slaves would be loyal to owners who treated them decently.

We might also recall the words of the Jewish sage Ben Sira quoted in chapter 1. Ben Sira urged slaveholders to do nothing unjust to slaves, yet he also encouraged corporal punishment to discipline wayward slaves. Ben Sira was hardly unique in pairing a warning against harsh behavior with an equally firm insistence on the disciplinary merits of beating slaves. Writing around 200 C.E., the Christian theologian Clement of Alexandria instructed slaveholders that torturing slaves was wrong. In the same passage, however, he urged them to apply the rod in discipline.[5]

Standards of behavior change. A century ago and even more recently, it was accepted that a parent's obligation to maintain discipline within the home required corporal punishment. "Spare the rod and spoil the child" was taken as timeless wisdom. Today, many acts of discipline have been widely reclassified as child abuse.

The household code in Ephesians is adapted from that in Colossians. Variation in instructions to slaves and slaveholders is minimal. What most distinguishes the advice in Ephesians and Colossians from parallel passages in pagan sources is that the Christian sources articulate a theological basis for submission of slave to slaveholder.

In Ephesians, the household code reads in part, "Slaves, obey your earthly masters [*kyrioi*] with fear and trembling, in singleness of heart, as you obey Christ; not only while being watched, and in order to please them, but as slaves of Christ, doing the will of God from the heart. Render service with enthusiasm, as to the Lord [*Kyrios*] and not to people" (6:5-7). A more literal translation of the phrase "render service" is "be slaves"; enslaved Christians are actually admonished to "be slaves with enthusiasm"![6]

It is sobering to contrast this one-sided instruction with Paul's injunction in Galatians, "Through love become slaves to one another" (5:13). Ephesians insists on a master-slave hierarchy that Galatians deconstructs.

The Pastoral Epistles

Two other New Testament writings attributed to Paul instruct slaves through household codes. As I have noted, although Pauline authorship for Colossians and Ephesians is disputed, they are understood to represent very early stages of post-Pauline development. Almost all New Testament scholars agree that the Pastoral Epistles—1 Timothy, 2 Timothy, and Titus—date from a later period in church life. By the time the Pastoral Epistles were written, church offices had undergone a considerable period of development. On this basis, I believe that the Pastoral Epistles best fit what we know about church life in the second century.

The author of the Pastoral Epistles was preoccupied with authority within the church. He attempted to dictate minimal requirements for those who sought to become leaders. A prime qualification was that a leader should be able to manage his own household. Describing qualifications for the office of bishop, the author wrote, "He must manage his own household well, keeping his children submissive and respectful in every way—for if someone does not know how to manage his own household, how can he take care of God's church?" (1 Tim. 3:4-5). Efficient management of a congregation drew on the same skills as efficient management of wives, children, and slaves. A householder was expected to instill discipline and obedience in members of the household. If he became a church leader, he was expected maintain a similar kind of ordered hierarchy in the congregation.

Both 1 Timothy and Titus supply advice to slaves but do not tell householders how to manage their slaves. Nonetheless, because 1 Timothy speaks to Christian slaves who have "believing masters," we can be sure that slaveholders belonged to the communities that received these letters. In fact, 1 Timothy is keen to emphasize that baptism of slaveholder and slave does not alter the dynamics of subordination:

> Let all who are under the yoke of slavery regard their masters as worthy of all honor, so that the name of God and the teaching may not be blasphemed. Those who have believing masters must not be disrespectful to them on the ground that they are brothers; rather they must serve them all the more, since those who benefit by their service are believers and beloved. (6:1-3)

As I have noted, most early Christian writings, including writings of the New Testament, reflect the viewpoint of freeborn men. Some of those freeborn men were slaveholders. Others were indebted to slaveholders for patronage of various kinds. We might have a different appreciation for early Christian thought if enslaved Christians had left a written legacy.

We have asked whether baptism altered relations between slave and slaveholder. First Timothy admonishes slaves that baptism *should not* alter their comportment. On this view, baptism does not diminish a slave's obligation to exhibit deference. Indeed, baptism is said to *intensify* a slave's obligations if his or her owner is a fellow Christian.

Yet we may infer that this view was not universally held. It seems likely that the author of 1 Timothy had heard Christian slaveholders complain about slaves whose behavior and attitudes had changed after baptism. A slave who emerged from the baptismal waters to hear that among the baptized there were "no longer slave and free" might expect that formula to change behavior. This is admittedly speculative. Nonetheless, 1 Timothy hints that slaves and slaveholders heard the gospel of freedom differently.

The other Pastoral Epistle to address slaves is Titus. Instructions to slaves recorded in Titus reinforce the most fundamental stereotypes of servile behavior: "Tell slaves to be submissive to their masters and to give satisfaction in every respect; they are not to talk back, not to pilfer, but to show complete and perfect fidelity, so that in everything they may be an ornament to the doctrine of God our Savior" (2:9-10). In antiquity freeborn persons were encouraged to cultivate noble virtues like courage and self-control. Slaves were encouraged instead to cultivate obsequiousness. Christian writings like Titus did not challenge this double standard.

We find another remarkable witness to such thinking in an early second work known as the *Apocalypse of Peter.* Virtually unknown today the *Apocalypse of Peter* was widely circulated in antiquity. In it, a seer is given a tour of hell. In the seer's visions the wicked are punished in ways that conform to their misdeeds. Body parts involved in sinning are tormented. Among the horrors of hell in the *Apocalypse of Peter* are "men and women who chew their tongue without rest while they are punished with eternal fire. These, then, [are] slaves who did not obey their masters. This, then, is their eternal punishment."[7] The deceased slaves ceaselessly chew the tongues that had the effrontery to confront their owners. The most typical "sin" of the slave was to refuse to play the part of a slave happily. Thus, Titus articulates the most basic expectation for servile behavior: don't talk back—that is, don't be uppity.

The household codes in the disputed Pauline epistles consistently reinforce ancient norms and expectations for slaves and slaveholders. If we think about the dependence of the earliest churches on the hospitality of baptized slaveholders who permitted Christians to gather for worship in their homes, this is not surprising. The question is whether the gospel was thereby diluted.

It is easy to recognize the moral compromises of the first and second century. Much harder to discern are the moral compromises Christians make today for personal or institutional advancement.

Extracanonical Writings

Christian theologians in later antiquity quoted the household codes of the deuteropauline letters as the basis for their own advice to slaves.[8] Several Christian household codes from the same era appear in extracanonical works. Both the *Didache* and the *Epistle of Barnabas* address slaveholders.[9] In each the slaveholder is instructed not to act out of bitterness or irritation to male or female slaves, lest such irritable behavior prompt slaves to stop fearing God. Why would a slaveholder's angry behavior prompt a slave to lose faith in "the God who is over you both"? In the Roman world anger was understood to be inconsistent with the self-control expected of the freeborn man. It was widely believed that anger had a corrosive effect on the angry person (and, in particular, on the angry man). A slave would understand his or her Lord (*Kyrios*) Christ by analogy to his or her earthly lord or master (*kyrios*). A slaveholder's fit of pique would thus risk diminishing the stature of the heavenly Lord.[10]

Both the *Didache* and the *Epistle of Barnabas* comment that God's call is independent of a person's status. Such statements appear widely in early Christian literature. They are often taken as evidence that, on some spiritual level, Christians overcame the liabilities of slavery. As a corrective it is important to note that both the *Didache* and the *Epistle of Barnabas* admonish slaves to subject themselves fearfully to the earthly master, who is described as a replica of God.

Here we might contrast the words of Genesis, which declares that all humanity is created in the image and likeness of God. In chapter 4, we will consider a sermon by the great fourth-century theologian Gregory of Nyssa. Because all persons are icons of God, Gregory decries slaveholding. What kind of person, Gregory asks, would declare himself or herself worthy to buy or sell a slave who is the image of God? In the earlier *Didache*, however, the slaveholder is singled out as resembling the Lord God.

1 Peter

I have reserved discussion of the household code in 1 Peter until the end of this section because I find it at once so troubling and so moving. In the Pastoral Epistles, the submission of slaves exemplifies the kind of good management that would qualify a male householder as a church leader. In contrast the author of 1 Peter acknowledges that slaves may have to submit to excessive force. In 1 Peter the slaveholding household is not a model for the church. Nonetheless, slaves are encouraged to conform themselves to distorted dictates of their owners:

> Slaves [*oiketai*], accept the authority of your masters [*despotais*] with all deference, not only those who are kind and gentle but also those who are harsh. For it is a credit to you if, being aware of God, you endure pain while suffering unjustly. If you endure when you are beaten for doing wrong, what credit is that? But if you endure when you do right and suffer for it, you have God's approval. (2:18-20)

Details of the passage underscore the divide between ancient and modern perceptions of justice. Beating a slave for wrongdoing is seen as just. However, 1 Peter does not suggest that the slaveholder who beats a slave should be seen as a stand-in for Christ or for God. Rather, 1 Peter links the abused bodies of slaves to the abused body of Christ. The author of 1 Peter invites slaves to contemplate the wounds of Jesus in order to give them strength to endure their own wounds: "For to this you have been called, because Christ also suffered for you, leaving you an example, so that you should follow in his steps" (2:21).

Although 1 Peter singles out slaves in this passage, the message throughout the epistles is that *all* Christians should patiently accept their sufferings. The community as a whole seems at risk of persecution: "But even if you do suffer for doing what is right, you are blessed" (3:1). As a result, suffering slaves could be seen as models for the rest of the church, even as the suffering Christ is a model for all Christians. According to 1 Peter, Christ did not abuse when he was abused; he did not threaten when he was suffered (2:23). As a result, "by his bruises you have been healed" (2:24b).

Other household codes urge slaves to submit themselves to their owners as they submit themselves to Christ. They thus liken the will of the slaveholder to the will of Christ. The *Didache* and *Epistle of Barnabas* even present slaveholders as stand-ins for Christ. The argument of 1 Peter is distinctive in that slaves rather than slaveholders are compared to Christ.

The effect of the advice in various epistles may be similar. Slaves should submit docilely to slaveholders. Nonetheless, the underlying logic of the passages is different. Household codes in the disputed Pauline epistles and extrabiblical writings conform to slaveholding norms in a straightforward way. In contrast, 1 Peter offers grounds for condemning the system of slavery by inviting comparisons between the abuse of slaves and the passion of Jesus. Slaveholders in the Americas who wanted to impress on their slaves the Christian value of docility turned to 1 Peter as well as to other household codes. At the same time, 1 Peter helped some slaves to construct meaning out of their brutal lives.

Christians today who work with exploited populations—including Christians working in global campaigns against contemporary slavery—are unlikely to endorse 1 Peter's prescription that those who are oppressed should accept their sufferings with equanimity. Yet many Christians will take comfort in 1 Peter's emphasis on Christ's sharing in the depth of human pain. First Peter encourages Christians to recognize Christ not in the face of the master but in the face of the slave.

Voices of Slaveholders

Sometime in the mid- to late second century, a Greek philosopher named Celsus wrote a tract mocking both Christ and Christians. His writing no longer survives. Almost a century later, however, in the mid-third century, the Christian philosopher Origen wrote a reply to Celsus. As a result we are able to reconstruct significant portions of Celsus's plaint against Christianity.

In Celsus's view Jesus of Nazareth was a dishonorable, no-account huckster. During his lifetime, he surrounded himself with vagrants and ne'er-do-wells. Following his death, word about him spread among silly women and children and among the meanest denizens of the empire, including slaves. Celsus painted what he considered an unflattering portrait of Christianity in order to discredit the movement. Ignorant manual laborers who had just enough sense to keep their mouths shut in front of their masters instructed the children of the household in the secrets of Christianity. Lowlifes who wouldn't mouth off in front of respectable men incited wellborn children to disobey their fathers.

Celsus's impression of Christianity varied notably from the way I've described it in this chapter. How to explain the divergence?

It's useful to recognize that Celsus relied on negative stereotypes of his day. His description of Christians evangelizing base members of society has echoes in the writings of another second-century writer, the pagan satirist Lucian. In several works Lucian depicted pseudo-philosophers swaying weak-minded folk. In one of those works, a character representing Philosophy protests against wannabe philosophers who are really just charlatans:

> There is an abominable class of men, for the most part slaves and hirelings, who had nothing to do with me in childhood for lack of leisure, since they were performing the works of slaves or hirelings . . . . While they were following such occupations in youth, they did not even know my name.[11]

For Lucian a slave couldn't become a philosopher because his training in servile things left no time for higher-minded pursuits.

It is easy to see that Celsus and Lucian shared similar prejudices. For them any group that welcomed slaves was morally and intellectually suspect. However, Celsus's reliance on stereotypes does not completely void his insights. Many (not all) pagan cults separated slaves from freeborn persons. When Christian slaves and free persons gathered together for worship, they attracted attention. By pointing out that many Christians were of low social status, Celsus attempted to discredit Christianity. But he didn't fabricate the presence of slaves in the churches.

Then why do so many Christian writings from the first, second, and third centuries reflect the values of slaveholders rather than the values of slaves? In part Christian writings shaded toward a kind of conservatism in an attempt to protect Christians from the kind of negative press that surfaced in Celsus's writings. Elite Christians anxious to silence rumors that the movement was seditious happen to be the authors of most surviving Christian literature.

As a result we have a different view of Christianity if we heed the words of pagan detractors like Pliny or Celsus than if we study many classic Christian writings. Prime among those writings are second- and third-century apologies. Apologies belong to the Greco-Roman philosophical tradition. The apologist presents and defends a particular point of view, in part by offering a critique of opposing points of view. The goal of the apologist is to persuade readers of the rightness of the position defended.

Unlike Celsus or Pliny, Christian apologists did not emphasize the appeal of Christianity to women or slaves. Indeed, one recurring theme of the apologies emphasizes the prominence of slaveholders within the church. According to second-century apologists Athenagoras and Justin Martyr, in order to gain information about Christians, pagan authorities tortured slaves.[12] We have already encountered slaves tortured to get information about the Christian movement: the two women ministers tortured by Pliny. However, the apologists did not write about tortured Christian *slaves*.

Rather, the apologists claimed that pagan authorities tortured household slaves in order to glean information about their Christian *owners*. (Some of the slaves so tortured may have been Christians, but if so, this fact was omitted.)

Athenagoras and Justin differ in the details they relay about these incidents. According to Athenagoras, some Christians owned a few slaves, and some Christians owned many. Regardless of household size no slaves of Christian masters were willing to testify against their owners, even under torture. In contrast, Justin wrote, when tortured, the slaves of Christians falsely accused their owners.

New Testament scholar J. Albert Harrill rightly cautions against accepting either tale as a transcript of actual events. The apologists played into widespread stereotypes of slaves as "domestic enemies." Tension between slaveholders and slaves was believed to be inevitable. The violence regularly meted out by owners was occasionally countered by slaves who acted with lethal force. Slaveholders valued their slaves' loyalty. They feared their slaves' disloyalty. Well short of killing, a disloyal slave might steal or spread ugly rumors—true or false, it almost didn't matter—about the household.[13]

Such behavior by a slave was not explained in terms of the impossibly compromised situation of human chattel but in terms of stereotypes about servile character. As we have seen in our discussion of the household code in Titus, slaves were believed to be vicious, prone to malicious falsehood and casual theft. (Of course, even a slave's bid to secure his or her freedom through flight was reckoned as theft of property!)

As Harrill shows, although Athenagoras and Justin differed on details about whether slaves protected their Christian owners or betrayed them, both exploited elite prejudices about slaves. For Athenagoras it was remarkable testimony to the virtues of Christian slaveholders that slaves in Christian households were unwilling to lie about their owners, even under torture. For Justin it was no surprise that slaves were so weak as to lie under torture.

The Christian theologian Tertullian went still further in his depiction of the perfidy of slaves. Justin suggested that torture produced the venomous lies some slaves reported about Christian owners. Tertullian wrote that slaves were so eager to malign their blameless Christian owners that no torture was necessary. Rumors about unsavory Christian practices were allegedly afloat. Tertullian's explanation? The kind of slaves who peered through peepholes were also likely to invent scurrilous tales.[14]

It is thus helpful to have a pagan like Celsus remind us that Christian slaves would not have shared the agendas of their Christian owners.

The Freedman Pope

Slaves outnumbered slaveholders in the Roman Empire. We do not have anything approaching a census of the early churches, but surely there were more slaves than slaveholders among the Christians. Because of prejudice against slaves, critics like Celsus emphasized that many Christians were slaves. Tertullian, Justin, and Athenagoras identified with slaveholding perspectives. Sharing Celsus's cultural prejudices, they emphasized the role of socially respectable slaveholders in the churches. Our survey of second- and third-century Christian attitudes toward slaves would likely yield different results if we could overhear a second-century slave sharing the gospel with a fellow laborer.

Our knowledge of even the most prominent enslaved Christians tends to be filtered through the writings of freeborn men. From 218 to 223, the bishop of Rome was a former slave named Callistus. Callistus apparently died a martyr. Unfortunately, our chief source for Callistus's life and thought is the *Refutation of All Heresies* by Callistus's contemporary, his rival Hippolytus.

On Hippolytus's telling, Callistus was a blackguard. However, the story Hippolytus told was rife with stereotypes about slaves. The slave Callistus belonged to a Christian named Carpophorus. Carpophorus entrusted Callistus with funds to begin a kind of bank. The bank accepted deposits from the vulnerable—widows and orphans. The enterprise did not go well. For Hippolytus there was only one explanation. Thieving like all slaves, Callistus must have stolen the money. Hippolytus did not consider the possibility that Callistus was simply a bad businessman.

When Carpophorus learned of the loss of funding, Callistus attempted to escape his clutches, thus confirming another ancient stereotype about slaves: given a chance, slaves flee their owners. According to elite ancient standards, Callistus's attempted flight was evidence of bad character.

When Carpophorus regained control of Callistus, the Christian master made sure the slave was subject to harsh corporal punishment. Fellow Christians pleaded for Callistus's release so that he could endeavor to repay the lost funds. As the tale continues Callistus is pictured as adept only in trickery. According to Hippolytus, Callistus relied on various forms of chicanery to improve his position and eventually to secure his freedom.

Hippolytus did not bother to narrate Callistus's ascent within the Roman church to the position of bishop. The two men had significant theological differences. In particular, Callistus was more lenient than Hippolytus in accepting the penitence of those who violated norms of sexual immorality, including adultery. In Hippolytus's list of Callistus's moral laxities, he included one telling item: the freedman bishop believed that women should be able to marry whom they liked. Specifically, a freeborn woman should be able to marry a male slave. Hippolytus was horrified. It was a violation of Roman law for a freeborn woman to marry a slave (a law that would be upheld even in post-Constantinian times) and a travesty in Roman custom.

Perhaps Callistus was a bad man who snaked his way into the Roman episcopacy. However, Hippolytus's account does not allow us to render dispassionate judgment. In his worldview, to permit a freeborn woman to marry a slave was the worst kind of moral lassitude. He did not tell the story of the freedman bishop as a vindication of the gospel of freedom. Rather, in his view, the fact that Callistus had been a slave was proof of bad character.

If we accept our written sources at their word, we would conclude that Christians, represented by Hippolytus, reaffirmed the traditional Roman condemnation of freeborn women who partnered with slaves. The record allows an alternate view. In the early third century, a bishop of Rome rejected ancient prejudices that barred unions between freeborn women and slaves. In this important domain he seemed to believe that legal distinctions between free and slave were irrelevant for defining relations among Christians. Surely, many Roman Christians appreciated this stance of the former slave who was their bishop.

Other Voices

Where can we detect the voices and concerns of Christians who questioned the hierarchies of the Roman Empire? Among our sources for early Christian attitudes are the works known as the Apocryphal Acts of the Apostles. Dating from the second and third centuries, these rambling fictions include fantastic yarns of miracles and conversions performed by the apostles. The Apocryphal Acts include elements sometimes characterized as gnostic. Regardless of the aptness of the gnostic designation, the works are indisputably Christian.

Like other early Christian writings, the Apocryphal Acts do not attempt a coherent analysis of the institution of slavery. Nonetheless, from their rich (and often fanciful) descriptions of slaveholders and slaves, we can infer something of their authors' attitudes toward Christians of varying social backgrounds.

Along with the apostles, who play starring roles, leading characters in the Apocryphal Acts are typically leading men and women of various cities of the Roman Empire and beyond. Narrative conventions in the Apocryphal Acts play on stereotypes of masters, mistresses, and slaves.

For example, in the *Acts of Thomas*, a wealthy woman named Mygdonia seeks baptism by the apostle. She calls on the services of a slave named Marcia, who nursed her as a baby and has served her faithfully ever since. Mygdonia's call for Marcia's assistance is a sentimental request evocative of many other intimate scenes between freeborn women and their faithful slave nurses in ancient literature. Asking Marcia to "have regard for her free birth," Mygdonia asks the nurse for a loaf of bread, water, and oil to be used in baptism and Eucharist.[15] Filled with fear when she hears God's voice at the moment of baptism, Marcia also begs to be baptized.

Yet despite the stereotypic depiction of the faithful slave loyally serving her adult ward, *Acts of Thomas* elsewhere evinces a critical attitude toward slaveholding. When we first encounter the slaveholder Mygdonia, she is riding on a litter carried by her slaves. Other slaves walk ahead of the litter to shoo away the crowds. The apostle Thomas addresses the slaves who carry the heavy litter. "You are those who carry burdens grievous to be borne, and are driven onward by her [Mygdonia's] behest. And although you are men they lay burdens upon you, as upon the irrational beasts, because your lords think that you are not men like themselves."[16]

Before the judgment seat, Thomas suggests, neither rich nor poor, slave nor free has an advantage. He invokes a version of the golden rule: "What is displeasing to us when done to us by another we should not do to another man." In a context where Thomas speaks directly to slaves who literally carry heavy burdens, such words are an implicit criticism of slaveholding.

Similar tensions play out elsewhere in the Apocryphal Acts, albeit unevenly. Christian slaveholders continue to command their slaves, yet there are repeated suggestions that adherence to the gospel should make a difference in the behavior of slaveholders.

Acts of Andrew includes a bizarre episode in which a married Christian slaveholder named Maximilla decides to live a life of celibacy. Maximilla sends her slave Euclia to impersonate her in the marital bed. The tale illustrates an aspect of slavery we will explore in depth in chapter 4, the sexual exploitation of slaves. Euclia's story is a gruesome cautionary tale. Irked by Euclia's boasting about the favors she receives from Maximilla for her part in the ruse, Euclia's fellow slaves reveal the deception to Maximilla's husband Aegeates. He responds by torturing and killing not only Euclia but also the slaves who reported on her behavior. Judgmental toward the slave Euclia for preening, *Acts of Andrew* is oddly accepting of Maximilla's exploitation of a slave.

Still, *Acts of Andrew* applauds elite figures who eschew privileges associated with their high status. Aegeates has a brother Stratocles, who becomes a Christian. Stratocles's peculiar behavior is reported to Aeagetes: "Even though he owns many slaves, he appears in public doing his own chores—buying his own vegetables, bread, and other necessities, and carrying them on foot through the center of the city—without shame in the sight of everybody."[17] Maximilla herself breaks bread with her slave Iphidama, a fellow Christian.

Acts of Peter suggests uncertainty regarding the compatibility of slaveholding with the gospel. The central action of *Acts of Peter* is set in the city of Rome. A senator has died, and his mother begs Peter to restore him to life. Peter hesitates. Manumitting slaves at the death of their owner was by no means a universal practice, but it was nonetheless a common practice. The senator's mother had already manumitted her deceased son's slaves.

Before Peter attempts to bring the senator back to life, he asks the mother, "'Those young men whom you set free in honor of your son, are they to do service to their master as free men, when he is [again] alive? For I know that some will feel injured on seeing your son restored to life, because these men will become his slaves once again. But let them all keep their freedom . . . , for your son shall be raised up, and they must be with him.'"[18] The mother assents. The incident creates a symbolic association between manumission and new life in Christ.[19] The slaves are born again when released from slavery, and the senator is born again when he is raised from the dead.

By no means do the Apocryphal Acts offer a straight-forward condemnation of slaveholding. The authors of the Apocryphal Acts draw back from the full implica-tions of the apostles' preaching. Nonetheless, there is a repeated sense that baptism should make *some* differ-ence in relations between slave and slaveholder.

Christianity Means Freedom

Let us consider a tantalizing possibility. The good news shared by early Christians was a word of freedom. Yet again and again it seems that Christian writings tamp down expectations that that word should be lived in a way that altered relations between slaves and slave-holders. But perhaps some Christians *did* understand there to be a connection between the gospel and libera-tion from human bondage.

In the early second century, the bishop Ignatius wrote a letter to a recipient named Polycarp that includes the following instructions to slaves and slaveholders: "Do not behave arrogantly towards slaves, either male or female. But let them not be puffed up. Rather, let them be enslaved all the more to the glory of God, so that they may happen upon a greater freedom from God. Let them not desire to be manumitted out of the money in the common chest, so that they may not be found slaves of [their] greed."[20]

By now, parallel admonitions to both slaves and slaveholders to avoid overbearing or arrogant behavior should not be surprising. In the household codes such advice was typically paired with injunctions to slaves to submit gladly to their owners. Yet Ignatius's letter goes in a different direction. He does not issue vague advice about proper Christian comportment in circumstances of servitude. Rather, and quite specifically, he discourages slaves from seeking to be manumitted out of a "common chest." What is he referring to?

As so often we wish we knew more, yet we can make reasonable surmises based on what we do know. Apparently, (some) congregations had a common treasury. Furthermore, (at least a few) congregations had drawn on those funds to secure the freedom of enslaved members of the congregation. Ignatius opposes the practice. It's easy enough to imagine that a small congregation would quickly run through its funds if it attempted to buy the freedom of *all* baptized slaves, yet this is not the reason Ignatius specifies. Instead, he is concerned that such a practice motivates the baptized to become "slaves of greed." Perhaps he fears that some slaves might seek baptism for the (sole) reason of manumission.

We should not exaggerate Ignatius's opposition. His words might fortify congregants reluctant to devote common funds for such a purpose. However, he does not criticize churches that choose to expend funds in this manner. Rather, he discourages slaves from seeking to secure liberty at congregational expense.

The good news here is not Ignatius's attitude. Rather, the good news is the suggestion that at least some Christian congregations understood freeing slaves as a common good.[21] Christians—not all Christians but some—seem to have acted on the premise that divisions between slave and free should not characterize relations among those who called themselves brothers and sisters.

To Live and Die for Freedom

In the second and third centuries, Christians told each other stories about those who died for the faith. Those stories commemorated slaves as well as slaveholders. Speaking and writing about martyrdom was an important way that early Christians crafted a communal identity.[22] It is sometimes said that the blood of martyrdom washed away differences between free and slave. This does not seem quite accurate to me. In the stories traded about martyrs, slaveholders and slaves retain their statuses even as they stand bravely before their executioners.[23]

Nonetheless, it seems important to me that Christians came to understood who they were as a community in part through stories they told about slaves. Executed in Gaul in 177 c.e., Blandina was the most memorable of slave martyrs. Writing in the fourth century, the church historian Eusebius preserved the account of her death:

> Blandina was hung on a post and exposed as bait for the wild animals that were let loose on her. She seemed to hang there in the form of a cross, and by her fervent prayer she aroused intense enthusiasm in those who were undergoing their ordeal, for in their torment with their physical eyes they saw in the person of their sister him who was crucified for them.[24]

According to this account, when spectators gazed on the tortured body of the slave, they saw the crucified Christ. As in 1 Peter, Christ was imaged in the battered body of the slave.

Telling stories about martyred slaves did not prompt Christian slaveholders to release their slaves. In writing about Blandina, Eusebius did not forget that she remained a slave. Rather, he insisted on her servile identity, even as he pushed his readers to recognize in her both Christ and the shared destiny of those who belong to Christ.

In daily practice, baptism did not appreciably change relationships between slaveholders and slaves. Nonetheless, those who embraced Christianity at times evinced a troubled awareness of the tension between the hierarchy of their world and the demands of the gospel. In Eusebius's account of Blandina's death, the irony that a slave represents Christ stands as a challenge, especially to those among the elite who would normally be taken aback at such identification. The reader is led to desire to be more like the slave, to be more like Christ.

We have seen that one strand of Christian morality enjoined slaves to obey their masters (*kyrioi*) as they would the Lord (*Kyrios*) Christ. Other strands of Christian discourse likened Christ not to master but to slave. Christians from the first centuries did not leave us written condemnations of slavery. However, they recognized Christ in the faces of those who suffered. This recognition is shared by today's Christians, motivating many to campaign against slavery and other forms of oppression around the world.

4

Slavery in a Christian Empire

The first generations of Christians were not in a position to affect Roman imperial policy regarding slavery. The situation changed in the fourth century. In 313 C.E., the emperor Constantine issued the Edict of Milan, which proclaimed that the practice of Christianity would be tolerated throughout the Roman Empire. No longer were Christians a persecuted sect. Over the next century large numbers of powerful men and women associated themselves publicly with the church.

In this chapter we consider whether, and in what ways, the growing power of the church affected the behavior of slaveholders and the lives of slaves. We also ask how Christian theologians managed to reconcile the realities of slavery with the preaching of the gospel.

I will continue to suggest ways that this history is important for Christians in the twenty-first century. In antiquity, only the rare Christian perceived the gospel to be incompatible with the institution of slavery. We may well wonder today what the gospel demands of us that we have failed to understand or to act on. But the news is not all bad. I hope the words and actions of some ancient Christians—admittedly few but nonetheless some—may inspire others to speak and act today.

The tension between proclamation and practice can be seen in the writings of Lactantius, a Latin-speaking North African theologian whose career spanned the late third and early fourth centuries. He declared that although some Christians retained the status of slaves, there were ultimately no slaves among Christians. Christians knew one another as brother and sister and as fellow slaves.[1]

Yet for Lactantius that declaration had oddly few consequences for everyday life. Not only did he expect that Christians would continue to buy and sell fellow Christians as slaves, he also insisted that justice required slaveholders to beat their disobedient slaves. Lactantius imagined a slaveholder who owned two slaves, one obedient and the other disobedient. Failure to beat the disobedient slave would be unfair to the obedient slave. Furthermore, Lactantius said, the slaveholder would be not only unfair but also foolish. Beating a disobedient slave educated other household slaves about what would happen to them if they stepped out of line.[2]

As an example Lactantius told a story of a slaveholder named Archytas. When Archytas discovered that his slave overseer had permitted a field to go to ruin, Archytas was merciful. He did not beat the slave overseer. Lactantius criticized Archytas on the grounds that slaves required punishment to keep them from grosser failings. Lactantius also contrasted Archytas's merciful treatment of his slave and parallel treatment of a freeborn person. In Lactantius's view if Archytas had restrained himself from expressing his anger at a citizen who offended him, he would merit praise.[3]

In the writings of one Christian theologian, then, we find succinct expression of a central paradox pervading ancient Christian writings on slavery. By and large the common affirmation that Christian relationships transcended distinctions between slaveholder and slave did not alter the actions of slaveholders. Nor is there evidence that the growing influence of the church appreciably improved the lot of slaves.

There were exceptions. We will pay attention both to the persistence of slaveholding practices and to the words and deeds of a few who took exception to those practices. What enabled those prescient few to break free from established patterns of thought and so articulate a distinctive—and distinctively Christian—moral vision?

Elite Slaveholders

The writings of fourth-century theologians tend to reflect the perspectives of the Roman Empire's elites. Christianity had an undeniable influence on the lifestyles of many upper-crust folk. Ascetic ideals inspired wealthy men and women to forgo worldly pleasures, including rich foods, soft clothes, and even regular baths. This did not mean the ruling class freed their slaves en masse. The privileged might choose to eat rougher victuals, but they were unlikely to shop for their own produce or bake their own bread.

Among elites, life without the assistance of slaves was simply unimaginable. John Chrysostom, the archbishop of Constantinople, urged Christians not to indulge themselves with large staffs of slaves—one or two slaves should be sufficient. We may surmise that John preached not to slaves but to their owners. John did not express concern for the impact of slavery on slaves themselves. Rather, he perceived excessive reliance on slaves to be harmful to slaveholders.[4]

Christian preachers urged their wealthy congregants to be mindful of the poor and the hungry. Even more

frequently, they urged their privileged listeners to cultivate personal humility. To enact such humility, wealthy
men and women sometimes slept on rough beds and
stayed away from the warmth of the steamy baths. Life-
style changes had the potential to introduce the slaveholder to some deprivations of a slave's life, but they
did not make life any easier for a hungry, tired slave.

Violence

Slaveholders sometimes heard words of criticism from
the pulpit. Excessive violence toward slaves was condemned. Preachers were aware that Christians as well
as pagans were capable of abuse. We should again
recall that decrying abuse did not entail a repudiation
of corporal punishment.

For example, John Chrysostom viewed the physical
discipline of slaves as inevitable, not only for keeping good order in the household but also for the moral
improvement of the slave. At the same time he painted
a scene of indulgent violence that he regarded as
unseemly for Christian slaveholders. He railed against
women who invited their husbands to watch as female
slaves, stripped and bound, were whipped with such
severity as to leave lasting marks.[5]

John's words are so graphic that the reader may
fear there was an unprecedented rash of pornographi-
cally bloodthirsty Christian women in major eastern
cities of the Roman Empire. Probably not—John's
words echo Roman caricatures of feminine excess. At
the same time neither should we dismiss his charac-
terization out of hand. In the early fourth century, a
church council at Elvira in Spain specified the proper
penalty for a Christian woman who beat her female
slave to death: for an intentional death, seven years

of excommunication, and for an unintentional death, five years. As New Testament scholar Bernadette Brooten points out, the penalty for a woman who killed her slave was less severe than the penalty faced by a wife who committed adultery or left her husband.[6]

Heavy metal slave collars are chilling artifacts of ancient slavery. Such collars were used to control and humiliate fugitive slaves and other slaves considered troublesome. Most surviving examples are post-Constantinian, and of these, many are marked with Christian symbols such as the alpha and the omega or the chi-rho. Nineteenth-century scholars were so disturbed by this evidence of Christian brutality that they referred to the objects as dog collars.

It has been suggested that Christians relied on the heavy metal collars in large measure because Constantine prohibited the long-standing practice of branding runaway slaves on the face.[7] Perhaps. Nonetheless, it seems that baptism had minimal impact on the disciplinary practices of the average Christian slaveholder.

Sex and Slavery in the Roman Empire

Throughout antiquity, slaves were the sexual property of their owners. For untold numbers of women, girls, boys, and young men, vulnerability to the sexual desires of their owners was central to the experience of enslavement. Furthermore, most prostitutes in the Roman Empire were slaves. Those who campaign against slavery in the contemporary world can unfortunately testify to the ongoing realities of prostitution and other forms of sexual exploitation for those in bondage. Human trafficking is a centerpiece of many twenty-first-century campaigns against slavery and other forms of forced labor.

We do not know how most slaves felt about their owners' sexual advances. It's easy to imagine that many slaves were unhappy to service their masters sexually. At the same time we can speculate that other slaves used the situation to their own advantage. The master's current favorite might enjoy better food, privileges for her family members, and lighter labor.

How widespread was the sexual use of slaves? Throughout Greek and Roman literature, the assumption that slaveholders had regular, casual sex with their slaves was unquestioned. In a survey article on sexuality in the Roman Empire, classicist Amy Richling even writes, "Respectable women's self-definition seems to have depended on sexual self-differentiation from slave women."[8] That is, freeborn women were in a position to say no to sex. Enslaved women did not enjoy that privilege.

A tidbit from the important early third-century compilation of Jewish law known as the Mishnah brings the point home. The Mishnah distinguished the marriage of a female virgin from the marriage of a sexually experienced woman. Converts, former captives, and freed slaves could not marry as virgins. The Mishnah specifies an exception. A girl born into slavery and freed before age three could marry as a virgin. Why? The rabbis believed that a hymen ruptured before age three could regenerate itself.[9] I don't think that such very young slaves were typically the sexual playthings of their owners, but the implication is clear. It was simply assumed that a female slave had been subject to predatory sexual behavior that she had not been in a position to resist.

Surely, we may think, if Christianity had any impact on the behavior of slaveholders, and thus the lives of slaves, it must have involved the sexual use of slaves.

Is this the case? Sources from the first few centuries of Christianity are virtually silent on the topic. New Testament scholar Carolyn Osiek speculates on possible reasons for the silence. Did writers in the first and second centuries "not speak of sexual exploitation of one's slave because a prohibition was self-evident (unlikely), because it was not done by Christians (also unlikely given the prevailing acceptance in the culture), because it was too much of a problem to tackle . . . or because they did not consider it a problem?"[10]

As we have seen at some length, ancient Christians generally considered it morally unproblematic—and in some cases, morally obligatory—for a slaveholder to beat a slave. Strange as it may seem, many Christians may have been equally accepting of a male slaveholder's right to use his slaves sexually. It is often noted that the first Christians absorbed sexual norms from Jewish practice. In that context it's important to remember that Judaism accepted a male slaveholder's sexual rights to his female slaves as a matter of course. Jews and Christians shared the same prohibition against adultery. For Greeks, Romans, and Jews, however, adultery involved sex between a married woman and a man who was not her husband. A married man could have sex with a slave, prostitute, or other available woman—a divorcee, for example—without committing adultery.[11] Whether pagan or Jewish, Christian converts had grown up with these cultural norms. In the absence of evidence to the contrary, it is reasonable to think that many of them would have continued to abide by those norms. In 1 Corinthians 7, Paul urged that sexual activity should be limited to marriage.[12] We may expect that many Christians absorbed Paul's lesson. But evidence from the fourth century and beyond suggests that the lesson was not universally learned.

Christian Sex

The third-century *Apostolic Tradition* of Hippolytus of Rome listed categories of persons whose baptism was prohibited or otherwise regulated. The document specifically considered the case of an enslaved concubine. She was eligible for baptism if she was faithful to her master and raised his children. A man with a concubine was eligible for baptism only if he entered into a legitimate marriage (not necessarily with his former concubine).[13] However, Christian writings from the fourth century suggest that not all Christians considered such regulations binding.

Some did. The great Latin theologian Jerome expected Christian men to abstain from sex with their slaves. He contrasted the behavior of Christian men with that of other Romans: "Free permission is given to lust to range the brothels and to have slave girls, as though it were a person's rank and not the sexual pleasure that constituted the offense. With us what is unlawful for women is equally unlawful for men."[14]

However, Jerome seems to have been in the minority in his understanding that all Christians shared his moral code. In contrast John Chrysostom acknowledged that Christians typically conformed to the sexual norms of the wider culture. In his preaching, he warned his congregants that a man who had sex with a slave was as guilty as a man who had sex with the empress. He nonetheless admitted that his words, which would surprise his hearers, would likely go unheeded.[15]

Nor were John's admonitions to Christian men to refrain from sex with slaves necessarily high-minded. John instructed Christian men to stay away from prostitutes, and most prostitutes were slaves. His rationale is a bit startling. You would not put on a garment previously worn by your slave, Chrysostom noted, because of the filthiness of the garment. So why would you be willing to share a woman with the same unclean slave?[16]

In warning against sexual use of slaves, theologians primarily expressed concern for the well-being of male slaveholders. By the fourth century sexual abstinence was enshrined as a Christian ideal. Marital fidelity was prescribed for those not inclined toward total abstinence. In contrast little concern was shown for the multitude of slaves who were routinely sexually coerced by owners, both Christian and pagan.[17] Although sexual abstinence was an ideal, female slaves were hardly likely to be permitted to choose celibate lives.

Basil of Caesarea represents an exception to this general rule. (We will hear more about Basil later in this chapter, as he was a member of a Christian family with a remarkable track record with respect to slavery.) He puzzled at differences in the human condition—"why one man is a slave, another free, one is rich, another is poor, and the difference in sins and virtuous actions is great: she who was sold to a brothelkeeper is in sin by force, and she who immediately obtained a good master grows up with virginity."[18] Elsewhere he addressed the situation of women forced against their will into sexual activity. Against the grain of much ancient thinking, he held that women who were sexually coerced should be considered innocent. He added, "Thus even a slave, if she has been violated by her own master, is guiltless."[19] Basil was rare in his explicit acknowledgment of the sexual burden borne by female slaves. Nonetheless, Bernadette Brooten points out, although Basil was aware of harm done to slaves, he did not penalize the sexually predatory behavior of Christian slaveholders.[20] In fact, as we will see, in time, Basil came to protect the rights of slaveholders.

If Basil provides an example of a theologian sensitive to the impact of sexual norms on enslaved girls and women, Bishop Ambrose of Milan typifies a straightforward identification with the moral perspective of the slaveholder. It's helpful to consider Ambrose's treatment of the sexual use of slaves in the context of his overall attitude toward slaves and slavery. As Ambrose developed his thinking on slavery, he referred frequently to biblical precedent. For him the patriarch Joseph proved that although a good man might be enslaved, he remained truly free in spirit.[21] Reduced to bondage by Pharaoh, Joseph remained the master of his own passions. Ambrose noted that Joseph's example might inspire Christians reduced to slavery through violence, as sometimes happened in the chaos of the Western Roman Empire in the fourth century.[22] Ambrose quoted Jesus' saying that the one who sins is a slave of sin (John 8:34) as he argued that the one free from sin was the only true free person. Slave might yet prove freer than slaveholder.

Such views might leave the impression that Ambrose saw legal enslavement as a matter of indifference, yet Ambrose's view was more complex. Citing the example of Esau, he argued that enslavement was a moral benefit to individuals who would benefit from a wise master.[23] At the same time, he did not believe enslavement was universally beneficial. In fact he incurred criticism for his use of church funds to purchase the freedom of Christians enslaved by force.[24] For Ambrose some people were naturally suited to life as slaves, while other people were not.

A distinction between persons naturally inclined toward servility or freedom underlies Ambrose's views on the sexual use of slaves. He treated the sexual use of slaves extensively in his discussion of the patriarch

Abraham. Like most Christian theologians Ambrose advised that sexual activity should be confined to marriage. At the same time his writing was shaped by older and still pervasive views on adultery. Sex with a slave might not be praiseworthy, but it was not as serious an infraction as sex with a freeborn man's wife.

Note that this formulation focuses only on the moral perspective of the slaveholder. Ambrose accorded no attention to the moral perspective of the slave, who might or might not be happy about her owner's advances.

Imagine the challenge that Abraham posed to the teaching that men should have sex only with their wives. The revered patriarch fathered Ishmael by Hagar, Sarah's slave. If Abraham could carry on with a slave, a man might ask, why can't I? In response Ambrose mounted several arguments. First, Ambrose simply urged men to satisfy their sexual urges with their wives. Second, Ambrose pointed out that women might cite their husbands' affairs with slaves in seeking divorce. (Ambrose did not support those women. He urged women whose husbands had sex with slaves to overcome their jealousy.)

Despite these arguments Ambrose knew that many Christian men saw nothing wrong with having sex with slaves and would continue to do so. His treatment of Abraham's relationship with Hagar ultimately focused on what he saw as the clear danger: that a slave favored by her master would become insolent to her mistress. Therefore, he insisted, men who slept with their slaves should take special care lest the household chattel get ideas above their stations.

As I've stated previously, Ambrose aligned himself in a singular way with the slaveholder's point of view. Nowhere did he give advice to slaves about how to handle sexual advances. Presumably he believed they *should* comply with a master's demands.

Yet in other contexts Ambrose wrote passionately about the moral good of resisting sexual advances. He praised the legendary Pelagia of Antioch. Threatened with rape Pelagia preserved her sexual purity by killing herself. Ambrose imagined the praiseworthy words Pelagia might have spoken: "I die willingly, no one will lay a hand on me, no one will harm my virginity with his shameless glance. . . . Pelagia will follow Christ, no one will take away her freedom."[25]

For Ambrose a free woman's sexual purity should be protected at the cost of death. He evinced no concern for the sexual purity of slave women. He certainly didn't advise Christian slaves to kill themselves instead of sleeping with their lecherous owners.

Although Ambrose's formulations are particularly striking, his views on the sexual use of slaves typify the views of other fourth-century theologians. Because men should confine their sexual activity to the marital bed, a man harmed himself when he slept with his slave. He also harmed his marriage. Theologians advanced no advice to Christian slaves beleaguered by sexual demands. Nor did they excommunicate men who frequented slave quarters.

As I have mentioned sexual exploitation continues to be a central dimension in many contemporary variations of slavery. Unlike fourth-century theologians concerned with the moral health of slaveholders, those who work today against human trafficking emphasize the costs of sexual exploitation to those forced into bondage. An important volume edited by MacArthur Fellow Bernadette Brooten examines slavery's impact on the lives of girls and women. With attention to both ancient and modern forms of slavery, *Beyond Slavery:*

Overcoming Its Religious and Sexual Legacies considers the legacy of slavery in Judaism, Christianity, and Islam.[26]

To heal the wounds of sexual exploitation, it is necessary to come to terms with the complicated ways that slaveholding norms infiltrated the moral codes of major ethical traditions. In antiquity Christian ethicists were attuned to the moral struggles of freeborn adult men rather than the ways that the behavior of freeborn adult men affected slaves and other vulnerable persons. In our own day we have become aware that church leaders have too often ignored the damage caused by adult authority figures to children and others in powerless positions. In particular Christian ethicists have too long been silent on sexual abuse of children by parents, members of the clergy, and other adults entrusted with care of the young. Attention to the blind spots of ancient Christian moral discourse can help us become more aware of blind spots in contemporary discourse and practice.

Why Slavery?

Calls for the abolition of slavery did not resonate in ancient pulpits, to say the least. But in carefully reasoned arguments, some theologians developed views that questioned the goodness of the institution. A number of theologians noted that slavery did not seem to be part of God's original design in creation. For example, John Chrysostom pointed out that God had not created a slave for Adam. Then why did God allow slavery to develop? In John's view slavery was a punishment for human sinfulness.[27]

A more complex version of this position was developed at length by the great North African theologian

Augustine. Augustine referred to Gen. 1:26: "Then God said, 'Let us make humankind in our image, according to our likeness, and let them have dominion over the fish of the sea, and over the birds of the air, and over the cattle, and over all the wild animals of the earth.'" God did not originally give human beings dominion over one another. Slavery was alien to God's creative plan.

Like John Chrysostom, Augustine understood slavery as a punishment for human sin. But isn't it unfair for one person to be born into slavery and another to be born as a slave? Augustine anticipated this objection. Because all human beings stand guilty before God, all are subject to punishment. God does not inflict punishment unjustly.

Slavery was thus a punitive institution. For Augustine it didn't follow that those who were enslaved were more deserving of this particular punishment than those who were free. Nor did slavery necessarily lead to the moral improvement of the slave. A good and wise person could be enslaved to a bad and foolish person. All this, Augustine argued, belonged to the fallen nature of the world.

Augustine believed that slavery was necessary to the peaceful function of society in a fallen world. In this sense, although slavery was a consequence of common human sinfulness, it was nonetheless ordained by God. The slave should accept his or her place in the social order, as should the slaveholder. The slaveholder was morally obliged to foster the good of those under his or her care. A slaveholder's judicious use of physical violence benefited not only the slave who was beaten but also other slaves who learned from the example.[28]

An episode Augustine records in his *Confessions* illustrates this perspective. According to Augustine, when his mother Monica was first married, malicious gossip spread by female slaves in the household poisoned her relationship with her mother-in-law. Monica responded with patience and equanimity. Eventually the mother-in-law was won over. She in turn made sure the slaves were beaten in order to dissuade them from fostering future acrimony. In Augustine's recounting of the tale, violence against slaves was the price justifiably paid for household peace.[29]

But not all Christians endorsed Augustine's commitment to slaveholding as a cornerstone of society.

Christians against Slavery?

Augustine maintained that the good slaveholder was more burdened by the responsibility of maintaining peace in the household than the slave by the obligation to submit.[30] Given this view it's not surprising that he was disturbed by the alleged actions of a group of Christians known as the Circumcellions. The Circumcellions were associated with the fringes of the Donatist Church in North Africa. Donatists understood themselves as the true Catholic Church, a claim rejected by imperially aligned Catholics. The Circumcellions had a reputation for violence, much of it enacted against members of the clergy. We wish we knew more about the Circumcellions. What we know about them comes from the writings of their opponents, a mix of invective and hearsay. We are thus uncertain of precisely what they did, much less why they did it. Nonetheless, we know enough to speculate that they took Jesus seriously when he said that the last would be first and the first last. They seem to have taken it upon themselves to bring that reversal about, at least in symbolic ways.

On a practical level it was reported that the Circumcellions destroyed documents that detailed ownership of slaves. Without such documentation a slave might successfully claim that he or she was a free person who had been kidnapped and sold unlawfully into slavery. The Circumcellions were also reputed to turn their violence against the persons of slaveholders. Like Augustine, Optatus of Milevis was a North African bishop aggrieved at the behavior of the Circumcellions. He wrote that because of the Circumcellions, the roads had become unsafe. In his words, "Even the safest journeys could not take place, because masters, thrown out of their vehicles, ran in servile fashion before their own retainers, who were sitting in their masters' places. By the verdict and bidding of those men the conditions of master and slave were transposed."[31]

Did such reversals in fact transpire? If so, what were the Circumcellions trying to accomplish? One scenario that fits the evidence is that the Circumcellions understood the practice of slaveholding to be incompatible with the promises of baptism.

Augustine wrote, "What master was there who was not compelled to live in dread of his own servant if he had put himself under the guardianship of the Donatists?"[32] It is important to remember that Augustine was not opposed to violence per se. After all, he supported the right of a slaveholder to exert violence against a slave. As we have noted he considered the judicious use of violence a slaveholder's obligation. However, for Augustine, it was crucial that violence should be used to support the social hierarchy, which he believed was in conformity with God's will. By the time Augustine wrote, the Roman Empire was in disarray, at least in the West. In several letters, Augustine decried the kind of social chaos that permitted kidnappers to steal free persons, whom they sold into slavery, a real risk in his world.[33] Those who were free had a right to freedom. Those in bondage had an obligation to submit. Those in power were equally obliged to use force to maintain order.

Although Augustine's may be the most memorable Christian voice from the era, his was not the only voice. We are able to learn about the voices of the Circumcellions only through the denouncements of those who silenced them. Nonetheless, the recollections of Optatus and Augustine prompt speculation about the motivations of the Circumcellions.

Were the Circumcellions unable to reconcile the practice of slaveholding with the liberating word of the gospel? Even if this is the case, the Circumcellions' reputation for thuggish violence casts a questionable light on their take on the gospel. We should at the same time remember that Roman slavery itself was dependent on constant and extreme displays of violence—violence condoned and at times applauded by major theologians of the fourth century.

No Longer Slave or Free

We have hints regarding another group of fourth-century Christians who were reputed to disrupt slaveholding relationships. They seem to have included a number of Christians associated with Eustathius of Sebaste, a leader in the monastic movement in Asia Minor in the fourth century. Christians in his orbit seem to have been troubled by the practice of slaveholding.

Once again, however, we lack documents composed by the followers of Eustathius. What we know about them is reconstructed from the documents of a fourth-century church council at Gangra, which condemned the partisans of Eustathius. The impression created by these documents is that those influenced by Eustathius had adopted an extreme form of asceticism.

The list of the group's alleged offenses is long. They were accused of vegetarianism and of fasting on Sundays instead of official fast days. The bishops at the council claimed that the followers of Eustathius condemned the rich who did not give away all their possessions, but did not acknowledge such condemnations as consistent with Jesus' own harsh words to the propertied. Married women were charged with refusing to have sex with their husbands. Some of the charges had to do with the appearance of these Christians. The women were said to cut their hair and wear men's clothing. Slaves were also accused of adopting strange dress, although we don't know what was distinctive about their attire. Moreover, the bishops claimed that slaves associated with the radical ascetic movement behaved contemptuously toward their owners and even fled from slavery.

The bishops who gathered at Gangra issued various condemnations related to the behavior of these renegade Christians. Regarding slavery, the council condemned anyone who encouraged slaves to flee their owners or even to behave contemptuously toward their owners. Such advice was mainstream Christian fare. Christians understood that Paul had returned the runaway slave Onesimus to his owner Philemon. The letter to Philemon was frequently cited as a mandate requiring Christians to return fugitive slaves to owners.

What is distinctive about the edicts emerging from the Council of Gangra is that they were issued to control the behavior of Christians who had different ideas about what it meant to follow the gospel. We don't know quite what those ideas were, as I've noted. However, taken together, the insinuations and mandates from Gangra hint at a coherent point of view informing the behavior of Eustathius's band of

Christian followers. Apparently, Christians influenced by Eustathius believed that the kingdom of God promised by Jesus was at odds with the hierarchies of the Roman Empire.

If we simply concentrate on the words of the bishops at Gangra, we will once again be led to the conclusion that ancient Christians believed the gospel was consistent with slaveholding—even that the gospel compelled Christians to support the institution of slavery. Yet let us remember that the followers of Eustathius were also Christians. Slaves who heard Eustathius preach took his message of freedom to heart, and some of their fellow Christians supported them. It seems that they attempted to live out the baptismal formula Paul quoted in Galatians: For those baptized into Christ, there is no longer slave or free.

In the Image of God

Eustathius was also influential in a prominent Christian family that included Basil of Caesarea, his brother Gregory of Nyssa, and their sister Macrina. Basil, Gregory, and Macrina are unusual in their attitudes toward slavery. They were not among Eustathius's more radical followers. After the bishops met at Gangra, Basil distanced himself from his former associate and teacher. Still, we may speculate that that the family had earlier been influenced by questions Eustathius raised about slaveholding.[34]

As noted earlier in this chapter, Basil had an unusual awareness of the costs of sexual exploitation for female slaves. After the Council of Gangra, in a period of reaction against Eustathius, Basil composed an extensive set of rules for monastic life. Those rules include a mandate to return fugitive slaves to owners, a requirement

in keeping with the bishops' words at Gangra.[35] But
Basil made an exception for slaves whose owners might
interfere with their adherence to the faith. Although
Basil retreated from what seems like an earlier sympa-
thy for the plight of slaves, we may nonetheless detect
formative contact with a Christian perspective that
called the rightness of slaveholding into question.

In his *Life of Macrina*, Gregory of Nyssa memo-
rialized his sister as a great ascetic, a wise and holy
woman. According to Gregory, Macrina convinced
their mother that they should not treat their household
help as slaves. Instead, they should all live together as
sisters. It is unclear whether the slaves were formally
manumitted; Gregory did not suggest they were. Gregory specified that Macrina and her mother shared bed
and board with their sister-slaves. He also described
the bed on which Macrina died as a sack spread over a
board. Although it's possible that Macrina moved from
a more comfortable couch as she approached her death,
it's probable that she simply died on the rude furniture
she shared with other members of the household. In
short, Gregory did not suggest that Macrina thought
to improve the living conditions of her sister-slaves.
Nonetheless, a decision to treat slaves as sisters suggests attention to the nuances of the gospel. Among
the baptized, there should be neither slave nor free.
Macrina understood that exercising the prerogatives
of slaveholding was at odds with her efforts to live a
Christian life. Perhaps she conceived this idea on her
own, or perhaps she was influenced by a family friend
named Eustathius.

Gregory of Nyssa composed what is probably the
most scathing critique of slaveholding in all antiquity. Perhaps he influenced his sister Macrina, or she
influenced him, or both might have been influenced

by Eustathius. Although Gregory made brief comments about slavery in several of his writings, his
most extended treatment of slavery appears in his
fourth homily on Ecclesiastes. The Teacher of Ecclesiastes wrote, "I bought male and female slaves, and had
slaves who were born in my house" (2:7). The Teacher
did not differentiate his possession of slaves from his
possession of other good things, including gardens,
vineyards, and flocks. But Gregory did. Although his
ostensible text was Eccl. 2:7, he was inspired by Gen.
1:27: "So God created humankind in his image, in the
image of God he created them; male and female he
created them." Genesis accords humanity dominion
over all the earth, including the fish of the sea, the
cattle of the field, and the birds of the air. Since each
person has dominion over the earth, Gregory asked,
how could any person claim dominion over another?
Gregory proclaimed that human nature was inherently
free. To enslave another person was to oppose God's
law. Human beings were intended by God to lord it
over lesser creatures, not over one another.

"I bought male and female slaves," said the Teacher
of Ecclesiastes. How much did you pay for them,
demanded Gregory. Which of your possessions did you
trade for a being endowed with reason? What could
you own that is equal in worth to a person made in
God's image?

Gregory continued his questioning, pointing out
both the absurdity and immorality of slavery. When
a slave was auctioned, anything he owned became the
buyer's property. However, Gregory pointed out, God
gave each person rights to the whole earth. What could
any buyer offer that was worth so much? And worth
even more, for a person's soul exceeded the value of
the whole world. God rescued humanity from sin. Why

would God look favorably on the enslavement of those whose freedom had been purchased at such high cost?

Gregory insisted that a bill of sale for a slave was a worthless and even deceptive document. What documentation could be given to record the transfer of the image of God from one master to another?

Earlier Stoics and Christians had insisted there were no ultimate differences between slaves and free persons. Gregory continued this tradition. Slaves and free persons were born in the same way and breathed the same air. Pain and sorrow afflicted both slaves and free persons, and pleasures touched both as well. Ultimately, both slaves and free persons would stand before a God who judged them.

Other writers who followed such a line of thought concluded by suggesting that legal status as slave or free was not of ultimate importance. Gregory came to a different conclusion. There is no difference between slave and free, he wrote. So how dare you claim to be master of another person, who, like you, was created by God in God's own image?

What is it that enables a person to break free from entrenched patterns of thought? In Gregory's case it was his engagement with Scripture. From Genesis he learned that each person is of infinite worth. His words resonate with startling clarity in the twenty-first century. We too live in a world where those created in the image of God are routinely degraded. Gregory's words remind us that we are all icons of God, endowed with reason and empowered to act.

Gregory stands out for the eloquence, vehemence, and coherence of his attack on slavery. But did he develop his position in isolation? He had contact with others whose words and deeds implied discomfort with slavery. I do not want to downplay what I see as

Gregory's genius. Instead, I want to suggest that we are unlikely to renew our moral visions all on our own. The struggle for justice is not a solitary undertaking.

I cannot say it better than Gregory. Oppression and exploitation are not only immoral but also blasphemous—insults to the image of God.

It is disappointing that so few Christians in antiquity perceived the profound wrongness of slavery.

It is inspiring that some did.

Epilogue

Why should Christians today care about the slave-holding environment in which the church first developed?

I have argued that, in insidious ways, slaveholding values affected the development of Christian thought and practice. Traces of those slaveholding values and priorities still affect us today. For example, early Christian theologians seem to us to be strangely indifferent to the impact of sexual exploitation on slaves, yet we are painfully aware how long such patterns of indifference have persisted in other guises. A generation ago, sexual abuse of children by parents, clergy members, and other authority figures was routinely hushed up. To correct the distorting traces of slaveholding values that linger in Christian thought and practice, we must first recognize them.

I often teach about early Christian slavery in my classroom and in parish settings. Inevitably, it seems, someone insists that Christian slaveholders surely knew deep down that owning another person was wrong. I don't think this is the case. Our moral instincts are profoundly shaped by our culture. I think that deep down most Christian slaveholders understood themselves to be responsible for the behavior of the slaves in their households. "Spare the rod and spoil the slave," they might have said.

One reason ancient slaveholders were wedded to slaveholding ideology is that they thereby profited. Like them we also profit from oppressive structures. Some ancient Christians—most memorably and coherently, Gregory of Nyssa—managed to stand back from the slaveholding system and declare it immoral. The ability to critique the moral system in which one has been formed is rare, but it is an ability that should be cultivated. I hope readers of this volume find themselves pondering the question of what systems in our world that we take for granted should in fact be challenged.

Jesus relied on everyday details in his parables. Not surprisingly, slaves and masters figure prominently in those sayings. Jesus also taught his followers that whoever wished to be first in the community must become the slave of all. Paul picked up on what I believe is a variant of this saying. He urged Christians to be slaves to one another. Although neither Jesus nor Paul turned away would-be disciples who were slaveholders, their teaching empties the slaveholding ethos of its power. As a thought experiment, it is worth considering how differently we might conduct our lives, individually and collectively, if we lived into the fullness of that teaching.

Like so many slaves in the ancient world, Jesus endured brutal beating. Crucifixion was a common means of executing slaves. As a result Jesus was said to "take the form of a slave." Through the ages Christians in hopeless circumstances have been comforted by this likeness; surely Jesus understands their suffering. *All* Christians are mandated to recognize Christ in the faces of the enslaved and the oppressed—and to work to end that oppression. Believing that the gospel promises freedom from all forms of bondage, some Christians are particularly inspired to participate in global campaigns against human trafficking and other contemporary modes of slavery.

Slavery exists in the world today. So do many other forms of degradation and exploitation. Gregory of Nyssa powerfully reminds us that each person is an icon of God and thus of infinite worth. Gregory denounced the arrogance of slaveholding. In antiquity to decry slavery was countercultural—and so will be our continued efforts to work for the dignity of every human being.

Further Reading

Bradley, Keith. *Slavery and Society at Rome.* Cambridge: Cambridge University Press, 1994.

Bradley, Keith, and Paul Cartledge, eds. *The Cambridge World History of Slavery.* Vol. 1, *The Ancient Mediterranean World.* Cambridge: Cambridge University Press, 2010.

Brooten, Bernadette J., ed., assisted by Jacqueline L. Hazelton. *Beyond Slavery: Overcoming Its Religious and Sexual Legacies.* Black Religion/Womanist Thought/Social Justice. New York: Palgrave Macmillan, 2010.

Callahan, Alan D., Richard A. Horsley, and Abraham Smith. *Slavery in Text and Interpretation. Semeia* 83/84. Atlanta: Scholars, 1998.

Corcoran, Gervase. "The Christian Attitudes to Slavery in the Early Church," *Mils* 13 (1984): 1–16 (part 1) and 14 (1984): 19–36 (part 2).

–––. *Saint Augustine on Slavery.* Studia ephemeridis Augustinianum 22. Rome: Gregorian University Press, 1985.

Garnsey, Peter. *Ideas of Slavery from Aristotle to Augustine.* Cambridge: Cambridge University Press, 1996.

Glancy, Jennifer A. *Slavery in Early Christianity.* Minneapolis: Fortress Press, 2006.

Harrill, J. Albert. *The Manumission of Slaves in Early Christianity.* Tübingen, Germany: Mohr, 1995.

–––. *Slaves in the New Testament: Literary, Social, and Moral Dimensions.* Minneapolis: Fortress Press, 2005.

Hezser, Catherine. *Jewish Slavery in Antiquity.* New York: Oxford University Press, 2006.

Klein, Richard. *Die Sklaverei in der Sicht der Bischöfe Ambrosius und Augustinus* [Slavery in the Views of Bishops

Ambrose and Augustine]. Forschungen zur Antiken Sklaverei 20. Stuttgart: Steiner, 1988.

Martin, Dale B. *Slavery as Salvation: The Metaphor of Slavery in Pauline Christianity.* New Haven: Yale University Press, 1990.

Patterson, Orlando. *Slavery and Social Death: A Comparative Study.* Cambridge: Harvard University Press, 1982.

Notes

1. Jesus and Slavery

1. See discussion in Catherine Hezser, *Jewish Slavery in Antiquity* (New York: Oxford University Press, 2006), 3–8.

2. J. Albert Harrill, *The Manumission of Slaves in Early Christianity* (Tübingen: Mohr, 1995), 172–78.

3. See discussion in Hezser, *Jewish Slavery in Antiquity*, 204–11.

4. Doubts have arisen about whether the Essenes actually repudiated slaveholding. The Dead Sea Scrolls, widely believed to be the work of the Essenes, include a text known as the Damascus Document. The Damascus Document suggests that slaves labored in Essene communities, although those slaves were the property not of individuals but of the community itself. How to account for this discrepancy? Perhaps Philo and Josephus were mistaken in the details they report about Essene life. Perhaps, as some scholars hold, the Essenes did not author the Damascus Document. Perhaps Essene practice changed between the composition of the Damascus Document and the time when Philo and Josephus wrote. For our purposes how the Essenes treated slaves matters less than their reputation for eschewing slavery.

5. Josephus, *Jewish War* 2.56, 68; *Antiquities* 17.271–72, 289.

6. Some scholars argue that the *pais* is the centurion's young male lover. See Theodore W. Jennings Jr. and Tat-Siong Benny Liew, "Mistaken Identities but Model Faith: Rereading the Centurion, the Chap, and the Christ in Mathew 8:5-13," *JBL* 123 (2004): 467–94. For reservations regarding

this proposal, see D. B. Saddington, "The Centurion in Matthew 8:5-13: Consideration of the Proposal of Theodore W. Jennings, Jr., and Tat-Siong Benny Liew," *JBL* 125 (2006): 140–42. Many slaveholders relied on slaves, male and female, as sexual outlets, so *pais* could simultaneously denote a slave and a (coerced or willing) sexual partner.

7. Joseph A. Fitzmyer, *The Gospel According to Luke X-XXIV, The Anchor Bible* 28b (New York: Doubleday, 1985), 1145.

8. Josephus, *Jewish War* 7.379–86.

9. See Moses I. Finley, *Ancient Slavery and Modern Ideology*, expanded ed. (Princeton: Markus Wiener, 1998), 95; and Keith Bradley, *Slaves and Masters in the Roman Empire: A Study in Social Control*, Revue d'étude latine 185 (Brussels: Latomus, 1984), 122.

10. Richard Saller, "Corporal Punishment, Authority, and Obedience in the Roman Household," in *Marriage, Divorce, and Children in Ancient Rome*, ed. B. Rawson (Oxford: Clarendon, 1991), 144–65.

11. In its immediate context, 10:41-45 stipulates expectations for *leaders* in the community. However, the pericope functions as a parallel to Jesus' specification of requirements for discipleship in 8:34-37. I therefore read Jesus' saying about voluntary adoption of the posture of a slave as having broad implications for Christian life and Christian community.

2. The First Christian Slaveholders

1. Regarding the circumstances that brought Onesimus to Paul in prison, still salient is the discussion in John Knox, *Philemon among the Letters of Paul: A New Vision of Its Place and Importance* (New York: Abingdon, 1959). For a strong defense of the traditional view that Onesimus was a runaway, see Margaret M. Mitchell, "John Chrysostom on Philemon: A Second Look," *HTR* 88 (1995): 135–48.

2. My discussion of the significance of family imagery in Philemon is heavily dependent on an important article by Chris Frilingos, "'For My Child, Onesimus': Paul and Domestic Power in Philemon," *JBL* 19 (2000): 91–104.

3. This question is well addressed in John Barclay, "Paul, Philemon, and the Dilemma of Christian Slave-Ownership," *NTS* 37 (1991): 161–86.

4. Barclay, "Paul, Philemon, and the Dilemma," 182–85.

5. http://www.africa.upenn.edu/Articles_Gen/Letter_Birmingham.html.

6. Space does not permit an extended discussion of Paul's attitudes toward women's roles in the churches. Even in 1 Corinthians 11, Paul tempers his comments on women's subordination by noting that "in the Lord woman is not independent of man or man independent of woman" (v. 11). The passages most frequently cited to suggest that Paul assigns subordinate roles to women appear in epistles whose authorship is disputed (Eph. 5:22-24; Col. 3:18; 1 Tim. 2:8-15; Titus 2:3-5). Many scholars also question whether Paul is responsible for 1 Cor. 14:34-35, which enjoins women to be silent during worship. Paul certainly had many female coworkers. See, for example, his extended greetings in Romans 16. Bibliography on Paul's attitude toward women is immense. Excellent starting places include Margaret Y. MacDonald, "Reading Real Women through the Undisputed Letters of Paul," in *Women and Christian Origins*, ed. R. S. Kraemer and M. R. D'Angelo (New York: Oxford University Press, 1999), 199–220; and Elizabeth A. Castelli, "Paul on Women and Gender," in Kraemer and D'Angelo, *Women and Christian Origins*, 221–35.

7. Peter Garnsey, "Sons, Slaves—and Christians," in *The Roman Family in Italy: Status, Sentiment, Space*, ed. B. Rawson (Oxford: Clarendon, 1997), 101–21.

8. For an argument that Paul refers to the Jerusalem *church*, see J. Louis Martyn, *Galatians: A New Translation with Introduction and Commentary*, vol. 33A, *The Anchor Bible* (New York: Doubleday, 1997), 457–66.

9. The most important exponent of this view is Dale B. Martin, *Slavery as Salvation: The Metaphor of Slavery in Pauline Christianity* (New Haven: Yale University Press, 1990).

10. New Testament scholar E. A. Judge even speculates that Paul was a slaveholder. "I have often wondered whether Paul himself had slaves," Judge wrote. "He ought to have had, because I do not really see how he could have traveled as he did without people to do the work." E. A. Judge, "St. Paul as a Radical Critic of Society," in *Social Distinctives of the Christians in the First Century: Pivotal Essays by E. A. Judge*, ed. D. M. Scholer (Peabody, Mass.: Hendrickson, 2008), 99–115, esp. 109. I disagree with Judge: surely if Paul had traveled with slaves, we would have some hint of that assistance in

his letters. Judge's musing nonetheless brings home the utter ordinariness of slaveholding in the first century.

3. Slaves in the Household of God

1. Pliny, *Epistles* 10.96.

2. *Shepherd of Hermas* Vision 1.1.1. We may infer that Hermas was exposed as an unwanted child (a common practice) and raised by a slave dealer (also a common practice).

3. J. Albert Harrill, *Slaves in the New Testament: Literary, Social, and Moral Dimensions* (Minneapolis: Fortress Press, 2006), 86. However, it should be noted that the agricultural handbooks primarily address elite slaves who managed estates.

4. John M. G. Barclay, "Ordinary but Different: Colossians and Hidden Moral Identity," *ABR* 49 (2001): 34–52, esp. 47–48.

5. Clement of Alexandria, *Christ the Educator* 3.12.93.

6. Harrill, *Slaves in the New Testament*, 90.

7. *Apocalypse of Peter* 11:6-9.

8. See, for example, Clement of Alexandria, *Christ the Educator* 3.12.95–96; and Cyprian, *To Quirinius: Testimonies against the Jews* 3.7.2.

9. *Didache* 4:10–11; *Epistle of Barnabas* 19:7.

10. See discussion in Harrill, *Slaves in the New Testament*, 94–97.

11. Lucian, *The Runaways* 12

12. Athenagoras, *A Plea for the Christians* 35.3; Justin Martyr, *Second Apology* 12.4.

13. Harrill, *Slaves in the New Testament*, 145–157.

14. Tertullian, *To the Heathens* 1.7.14–17; Tertullian, *Against Marcion* 5.6.7.

15. *Acts of Thomas* 120.

16. *Acts of Thomas* 83.

17. *Acts of Andrew* 25.

18. *Acts of Peter* 28.

19. For related discussion, see Judith Perkins, *Roman Imperial Identities in the Early Christian Era* (New York: Routledge, 2010), 159–62.

20. Ignatius, *Epistle to Polycarp* 4.3. Translation from J. Albert Harrill's crucial discussion in *The Manumission of Slaves in Early Christianity* (Tübingen, Germany: Mohr, 1995), ch. 4.

21. In this they would not have been unique. There is some evidence that Jews in the Diaspora purchased the freedom of enslaved Jews. See Harrill, *The Manumission of Slaves*, 172–78.

22. For a detailed argument, see Elizabeth A. Castelli, *Martyrdom and Memory: Early Christian Culture Making*, Gender, Theory, and Religion (New York: Columbia University Press, 2007).

23. Jennifer A. Glancy, *Corporal Knowledge: Early Christian Bodies* (New York: Oxford University Press, 2010), 56–61.

24. Eusebius, *Ecclesiastical History* 5.41.

4. Slavery in a Christian Empire

1. Lactantius, *Divine Institutes* 5.15.2.

2. Lactantius, *The Wrath of God* 5.12.

3. Lactantius, *The Wrath of God* 18.

4. John Chrysostom, *Homilies on 1 Corinthians* 40.6.

5. John Chrysostom, *Homilies on Ephesians* 15.

6. Personal communication from Bernadette Brooten.

7. Joyce Reynolds, "Roman Inscriptions 1971–5," *JRS* 66 (1976): 174–99, esp. 196. Alan Watson argues that legal changes under Constantine did little if anything to lessen violence against slaves. "Roman Slave Law and Romanist Ideology," *Phoenix* 37 (1983): 53–65, esp. 59–65.

8. Amy Richlin, "Sexuality in the Roman Empire," in *A Companion to the Roman Empire*, ed. D. S. Potter (Oxford: Blackwell, 2006), 327–53, esp. 350.

9. *Mishnah Ketubbot* 1:2D, 4C; *Mishnah Niddah* 5:4. See discussion in Judith Romney Wegner, *Chattel or Person? The Status of Women in the Mishnah* (New York: Oxford University Press, 1988), 21–23, and in Gail Labovitz, "The Purchase of His Money: Slavery and the Ethics of Jewish Marriage," in *Beyond Slavery: Overcoming Its Religious and Sexual Legacies*, ed. Bernadette J. Brooten with the editorial assistance of Jacqueline L. Hazelton (New York: Palgrave MacMillan, 2010), 91–105, esp. 97–98.

10. Carolyn Osiek, "Female Slaves, *Porneia*, and the Limits of Obedience," in *Early Christian Families in Context: An Interdisciplinary Dialogue*, ed. D. L. Balch and C. Osiek (Grand Rapids: Eerdmans, 2003), 255–74, esp. 274.

11. Among Greeks and Romans, a freeborn man also expected to have sexual access to young males.

12. For more a more complex consideration of how sexual exploitation might have affected slaves who sought baptism in the first century, see Jennifer A. Glancy, "Obstacles to Slaves' Participation in the Corinthian Church," *JBL* 117 (1998): 481–501.

13. Hippolytus, *The Apostolic Tradition* 16:14–16.

14. Jerome, *Epistles* 77.3.

15. John Chrysostom, *Homilies on 1 Thessalonians* 5.

16. Ibid.

17. For extended discussion, see Jennifer A. Glancy, *Corporal Knowledge: Early Christian Bodies* (New York: Oxford University Press, 2010), 60–74.

18. Basil of Caesarea, *On Psalm 32* 5.

19. Basil of Caesarea, *Epistles* 199.49.

20. Bernadette J. Brooten, "Introduction," in *Beyond Slavery: Overcoming its Religious and Sexual Legacies*, 1–29, esp. 10 and 23 n. 38.

21. Ambrose, *Epistles* 37. Other Christian theologians also relied on the example of Joseph to argue that true freedom was not defined by legal status.

22. Ambrose, *On Joseph the Patriarch* 4.20.

23. Ambrose, *Epistles* 77.6. Other Christian theologians also turned to Esau to argue that in some instances slavery was a moral benefit for the slave. Note that similar arguments were ultimately made by American slavery advocates, who suggested that pagan Africans had benefited from the Christianizing and hence "civilizing" legacy of enslavement.

24. Ambrose, *Epistles* 37.

25. Ibid.

26. Brooten, ed., *Beyond Slavery* (see note 9).

27. John Chrysostom, *Homilies on 1 Corinthians* 40.6.

28. For further discussion of Augustine's complex view on slavery, see Peter Garnsey, *Ideas of Slavery from Aristotle to Augustine* (Cambridge: Cambridge University Press, 1996), 206–19.

29. Augustine, *Confessions* 9.9.

30. Augustine, *City of God* 19.16.

31. Optatus, *Against the Donatists* 3.4.

32. Augustine, *Epistles* 108.6.18.

33. Augustine, *Epistles* 10* and 24*.

34. See Susanna Elm, *"Virgins of God": The Making of Asceticism in Late Antiquity* (Oxford: Clarendon, 1994), 135. See also Anna B. Silvas, *The Asketicon of St. Basil the Great* (Oxford: Oxford University Press, 2005), 57–58.

35. Basil of Caesarea, *Longer Rule* 11. See discussion in Silvas, *The Asketicon of St. Basil the Great*, 31.